This special edition of *Beaumont: A
Chronicle of Promise,* commemorating the
sesquicentennial of the city of Beaumont,
1837-1987, has been made possible through
the generosity of the following patrons:

Beaumont Eye Associates
The Beaumont Enterprise
First City National Banks

First City National Bank of Beaumont
First City Bank—Central
First City Bank—Gateway

Mehaffy, Weber, Keith, and Gonsoulin
T. E. Moor and Company
Ben, Sol, Nate, and Vic Rogers
C. L. Sherman and Sons, Lumber Dealers
The Texas Gulf Historical Society

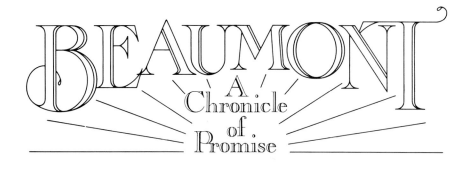

BEAUMONT
A Chronicle of Promise

Jan. 10, 1990

Best wishes,
Judith Walker Linsley
Ellen Walker Rienstra

For our father, John H. Walker

These young people posed during an excursion to Lake Sabine southeast of Beaumont. Left to right, front, are Vallie Fletcher, Carrie Bacon, and Henry Langham; middle, Will Keith, Ethel Leary, Kate and Marion Fletcher, and Earl Wilson; standing at the top, Jim Keith. Courtesy, Beaumont Heritage Society.

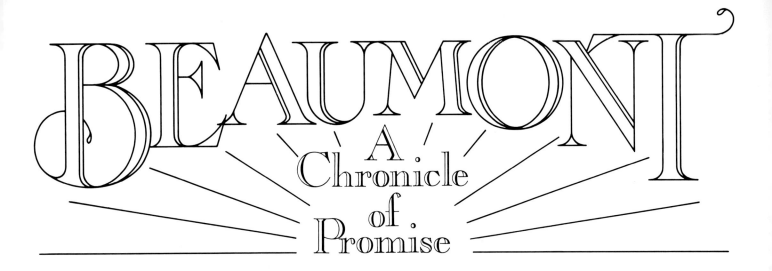

BEAUMONT
A Chronicle of Promise

An Illustrated History
by
Judith Walker Linsley & Ellen Walker Rienstra

Picture research by Wesley Norton
"Partners in Progress" by Robert C. Andrews
Foreword by Rosine McFaddin Wilson
Introduction by William Seale

Sponsored by the Beaumont Chamber of Commerce and
the Texas Gulf Historical Society

Windsor Publications, Inc.
Woodland Hills, California

Windsor Publications
History Book Division

Publisher: John M. Phillips
Editorial Director: Lissa Sanders
Administrative Coordinator: Katherine Cooper
Senior Picture Editor: Teri Davis Greenberg
Senior Corporate History Editor: Karen Story
Production Manager: James Burke
Art Director: Alexander D'Anca
Art Production Manager: Dee Cooper
Composition Manager: E. Beryl Myers

Staff for Beaumont: A Chronicle of Promise
Editor: Phyllis Rifkin
Picture Editor: Jana Wernor
Editorial Assistants: Phyllis Gray and Mary Mohr
Compositors: Barbara Neiman and Shannon Mellies
Proofreaders: Susan Gutierrez, Ruth Hoover, Jeff Leckrone, and Doris Malkin
Designer: John Fish
Layout Artists: Shannon Strull and Melinda Wade
Production Artist: Shannon Strull
Lettering: Janet Bailey

Library of Congress Cataloging in Publication Data

Linsley, Judith Walker.
    Beaumont, a chronicle of promise.

    "Sponsored by the Beaumont Chamber of Commerce
and the Texas Gulf Historical Society."
    Bibliography: p. 145
    Includes index.
    1. Beaumont (Tex.)—History. I. Rienstra, Ellen
Walker. II. Title.
F394.B3L56   976.4'145   82-70927
ISBN 0-89781-053-8   AACR2

Radio began in Beaumont when KFDM, owned and operated by Magnolia Petroleum Company, went on the air in October 1924. Broadcasts of such features as Harry Cloud's Magnolia Band originated from the cafeteria just outside the refinery gates until the station moved to the roof of the Hotel Beaumont and increased its power late in 1929. The band is shown standing in front of Beaumont High School. Courtesy, Business Men's Studio.

Table of Contents

Foreword

The introduction of a new history of Beaumont is an occasion for rejoicing. New historians, though they may seem to be plowing the same ground as their predecessors, look upon the territory from new standpoints, uncover new sources of information, emphasize different events and data, and make new interpretations of older material. History is not one simple set of facts, but complex, intertwined sets of facts, and different, often opposing points of view. Historians find that in their work they must be a combination of detective, advocate for many traditions and premises, and judge and jury on the evidence.

Ellen Walker Rienstra and Judith Walker Linsley have brought to this volume fresh energy and vision, extensive research, and their own deep-rooted heritage as sixth-generation East Texans and Beaumonters. New, primary sources of information have been brought to light to make this book a very valuable addition to Beaumont's historical lore. Accurate, unpretentious, and easy to read, *Beaumont: A Chronicle of Promise* should help to popularize local history with Beaumonters. It is a pleasure to recommend it to all.

Rosine McFaddin Wilson

Acknowledgments

A project such as *Beaumont: A Chronicle of Promise* is in one sense a community endeavor, necessarily involving many people other than its authors. Because so many contributed to its completion, either by furnishing vital materials or by simply offering their enthusiasm, it would be impossible to sufficiently acknowledge everyone's help. However, we must give particular thanks to a few.

For graciously sharing their family heritage with us, we are grateful to Chilton O'Brien, Jane Clark Owens, Zulieka Elizabeth Winslow Semans, Mary Clare Pye Wilsford, Lilla Frampton, Erin Barry Teare, Marie Rienstra Fleming, Eleanor Perlstein Weinbaum, Anthony Brocato, Mary Lou Ainsworth, Myrtle Sprott Deplanter, Velma White Caswell, Mamie McFaddin Ward, and Catherine Cokinos. Alan McNeill, Edna Brooks, Dwight Thompson, Beatrice Wright, Midge French, County Clerk R.L. Barnes, Haywood Walker, Betty Cuthrell, Aaron Davis, and Erin O'Brien volunteered in various ways their knowledge, materials, information, or time.

To Charlsie Berly and Dr. Winfred S. Emmons of the John and Mary Gray Library of Lamar University, to Maurine Gray of the Beaumont Public Library, to Mabel Leyda of the Tyrrell Historical Library, to Joyce Calhoon and Sheila Smith of the Sam Houston Regional Library at Liberty, and to David Hartman of the Spindletop Museum, we would like to express our deepest appreciation for their invaluable help, freely given. Yvonne Craig and Nell Truman of the John Jay French Museum also provided general assistance and, from the beginning, constant moral support.

Mayor Maurice Meyers, Chamber of Commerce Executive Director Dennis Sederholm, and attorneys Robert Q. Keith and Tanner T. Hunt greatly aided us in developing a perspective of modern Beaumont. Lissa Sanders and Phyllis Rifkin of Windsor Publications generously praised our efforts, at the same time giving us the benefit of their superb editorial skills.

Above all, to the members of the business community who are spotlighted in the Partners in Progress chapter, we are profoundly grateful for making this history possible. And a vote of thanks must go to Bob Andrews, who worked so diligently to prepare the biographies of these businesses and individuals.

Area historians, both amateur and professional, have spent many years researching the history of this corner of the world; their willingness to share this knowledge with us made our task much easier. For this generosity we would like to thank William Seale, Naaman Woodland, William Quick, W.T. Block, and especially Rosine McFaddin Wilson, who gladly volunteered her considerable expertise to ensure the accuracy of our manuscript.

To Dr. Wesley Norton, professional historian and photographer in the finest sense of the word *amateur,* we would like to express our profound appreciation for a job well done. With his photographs, he has given to Beaumonters a sensitive, affectionate portrait of their town. He was assisted in his search for illustrations by many, including Darrell and Wayne Baker, who graciously and generously made available their magnificent collection of photographs by Lloyd Baker. First Baptist and First Methodist churches provided extensive photographic collections. Mighty thanks also go to Stuart Hayes of Lamar University Photographic Services for his superb processing and his patience in the face of overwhelming numbers of pictures.

Our special thanks go to our husbands, Kenneth Linsley and John Rienstra, and to our children, Shannon Wilson, Ken and Sam Linsley, and Dan, Judy, and Allen Rienstra, who we are sure were convinced this project would never end, yet were unflagging in their support of it; to our mother, Esther Walker, and our housekeeper, Lena Chatmon, for many extra hours of assistance they rendered us, mostly in the form of babysitting; and to our cousin, Callie Wilson, who taught us a great deal about writing.

We dedicate this book to our father, John H. Walker, a lifelong resident of Beaumont, whose support of his hometown has been surpassed only by his encouragement of and pride in whatever his children have done.

Top left
The barbershop was next to the Nash boardinghouse on Pearl Street. Ed Ogden is the tallest of the men near the center of the picture. S.W. McCarty is leaning against the middle pole and J.D. Goodin, blacksmith, stands at the far right. Courtesy, Tyrrell Historical Library.

Top right
The new activity at Spindletop did not suppress the cattle business. In fact, expansion of the beef cattle industry in the 1920s nearly doubled production by 1930. Courtesy, Spindletop Museum.

Above
The Tyrrell Library bookmobile, shown here in 1929, was the first such service in Texas and one of the first in the nation. Lucy Fuller Gross instituted this service during her tenure as director from 1926-1933. Miss Pearle Burr and Miss Fuller are standing at right. Courtesy, Tyrrell Historical Library.

Introduction

To those who live in Beaumont, Texas, much of the city pictured and described in this history will seem to belong to another place. The townscape has changed greatly since the building boom of the 1920s established the city's well-known skyline. Progress, while ensuring a city's survival, often alters its ambience, however subtly. With the onset of the wrecking ball, much that was fine and familiar has passed away.

Former Beaumonters who are over say, forty, invariably remember, as I do, Calder Avenue and other fine old streets as they used to be. Faint traces of the residential flavor of those days lingers in the south end, on old streets like Orange and Irma, where gangly frame houses—nearly always painted white—slumber and sometimes lean wearily in overgrown thickets of old-fashioned shrubbery and vines, with an occasional palm. But for the most part that Beaumont is gone.

Downtown is gone too. I recall the hot, bright streets with their awnings, their cat's cradles of overhead electrical wires, their buildings nosing up against the concrete sidewalks. It was a busy place. In the very back of my desk drawer is a snapshot taken back in the '40s by one of the street photographers who worked Pearl Street on sunny days. It shows two women with armloads of packages, smiling, with hats and veils and white gloves, dressed for town as town used to be. Seeing it never fails to bring forth a rush of nostalgia in me.

Trying to describe Beaumont in all its intricacies and contradictions to people in faraway places is difficult. Beaumonters do love to talk about Beaumont, and one ends up talking until he is told, "You should write a book about the place!" Happily, Judith Walker Linsley and Ellen Walker Rienstra have done just that. Theirs is not a lament, but a celebration. The swift current of their narrative kindles the memory of those who know the town and will prove good reading to anyone else. The first of its kind to appear in nearly 50 years, *Beaumont: A Chronicle of Promise* is an affectionate account, beautifully written and illustrated, of a little city the likes of which is nowhere else to be found.

William Seale

Chapter I

The Promise of the Land

This is the most beautiful country in the world. . . .
— François Simars de Bellisle, marooned
in Southeast Texas in 1719.

A history of any city must begin with the land. Geography determines the livelihood of the first inhabitants of an area; it affects the quality of their existence as settlement progresses, and emerges finally as the arbiter of their way of life. A region rich in native resources makes to its people an implicit promise of a satisfying life, a pledge redeemable with forethought, hard work, and good faith. The city of Beaumont, Texas, located on a high bluff on the Neches River near its conjunction with the Gulf of Mexico, bounded on the southwest by vast prairies and on the north by the verdant, looming presence of the Big Thicket, lies at the convergence of choice lands, diverse in nature but alike in reward. The story of the settlers of this favored Southeast Texas spot and their success or failure in utilizing these riches is the story of the city of Beaumont.

The first people to avail themselves of the bounty of this land were its aboriginal inhabitants, the so-called "Paleo Indians," who came to this area about 12,000 years ago. For an indeterminate time they hunted the giant sloth, mammoth, and saber-toothed tiger that roamed the coastal prairies; then the Paleos vanished, leaving no trace of their existence except flint arrowheads, a few crude tools, and fossilized bones.

The next inhabitants of Southeast Texas were the Attakapas Indians, who migrated from Southwest Louisiana across the Sabine River approximately 2,000 years ago. This tribe, which also included the kindred groups of the Deadose, the Bidais, and the Orcoquisa, occupied the land from the lower Sabine, Neches, and Trinity rivers to the coast.

The Attakapas hardly fit the romantic stereotype of the "noble savage." They were a short, stocky people, with dark skins, coarse black hair, large heads, and features of "an unpleasant cast," according to an early observer. Furthermore, they smeared alligator oil on their bodies to repel the voracious swarms of mosquitoes that infested the area (a problem of which succeeding residents have often complained). Whether the oil repelled the mosquitoes is not recorded; what is emphasized, however, in more than one account, is that its extremely offensive odor repulsed the early explorers and missionaries.

Facing page
The ships of René Robert Cavelier, Sieur de La Salle, touched land near Sabine Pass on New Year's Day 1685 during his search for the Mississippi River. La Salle built Fort St. Louis near Matagorda Bay before setting off again on his quest. Courtesy, Institute of Texan Cultures.

Above
Always a primary source of food, the Gulf of Mexico became an important thoroughfare for the European explorers who settled in the New Land. Resources from the Gulf have since sustained each generation of residents along its coast. Photo by Wesley Norton.

Top right
Early humans used the large points in the top row of this photo to bring down mammoth or bison. These points date from the Paleo Indians—10,000 to 12,000 years ago. The Attakapas and later dwellers in the Beaumont area used the smaller points for lesser game and fish. Photo by Wesley Norton. Courtesy, Russell Long.

Above
The awesome alligator was utilized by the Attakapas for mosquito repellent and lamp oil. Later, Southeast Texas preachers riding through the swamplands reportedly supplemented meager incomes by selling alligator hides. The creature was to yield its hide to the white man almost to the point of its own extinction. Courtesy, Texas Parks and Wildlife.

Alligator oil was doubly important to this primitive culture, for it was also used in their lamps, which they made of conch shells and dried moss. Their household utensils included crude pottery, wooden bowls, gourd dippers, woven cane baskets, and containers made of skin. Tribal clothing consisted of breechclouts for the men and simple skirts for the women, all of deerskin, with perhaps a buffalo robe added for warmth in the winter. All went barefoot.

The name "Attakapas" means "man-eater" in the Choctaw language, and the Attakapas did indeed cultivate the unpleasant habit of eating other humans. Their cannibalism, however, like that of some of the other Texas tribes, seems to have been ritualistic rather than life-supporting; according to the graphic account of a young

French officer, François Simars de Bellisle, who was marooned for two years among the Orcoquisa, a slain enemy was devoured not only in order to acquire his strength but also to eternally damn his soul.

These Indians did little farming, being able to live almost entirely off the bounty of the land. However, their apparent laziness prompted the censure of Father Juan Agustín Morfi, an early Spanish missionary:

> *[The Attakapas] live at the mouths of the Nechas [sic] and Trinidad Rivers . . . ; they neglect the cultivation of their fertile lands, occupy themselves with and live from . . . the game which abounds in their forests.*

Children of the water whose tribal tradition included the story of an ancient flood, the Attakapas wandered sea-

sonally between the rivers and the coast in their search for food. In the spring and summer they expertly navigated the Gulf waters among the offshore islands in their dugout canoes. They shot alligators with bows and arrows, caught fish with spears or nets of woven brush, and easily gathered oysters, crabs, birds' eggs, plants, nuts, and berries in plenty. They also found washed up on the beaches sun-hardened slabs of crude petroleum from the ocean floor, which they used in making arrows.

In the winter the Attakapas moved inland to hunt and fish to the north. On the higher ground they built semi-permanent villages, two of which were located on opposite sides of the Neches in the vicinity of present-day Beaumont. In these villages the Indians constructed crude brush huts and raised huge mounds of oyster shells upon which they built the houses of their chiefs and shamans. (These shell

Top
Plain as they may seem, these beads found along the coast indicate that interest in ornamentation existed among the Attakapas. Photo by Wesley Norton. Courtesy, Russell Long.

Above
A sack of garbage from an Attakapas midden, or shell mound, near the Neches River reveals a diet including shellfish and deer flesh. The cook also left behind some broken pottery. Photo by Wesley Norton. Courtesy, Russell Long.

Above
Bluffs along the treelined Neches River first furnished natural campsites for Indians, then townsites for white settlers. Tapping the resources of the interior and flowing into the Gulf of Mexico 45 miles away, the river is ideal for commercial and recreational interests. This photo was taken from the site of the historic Collier's Ferry. Photo by Wesley Norton.

piles were apparently also used as garbage dumps and burial sites; Joseph Grigsby, a 19th-century planter who settled on the Neches a few miles south of Beaumont, leveled ancient mounds on his property which were found to contain shards of pottery and human bones.)

A short distance upriver from the Attakapas villages were the great stands of East Texas pine and hardwood forests. These woods merged northwestward into the heavy timber, tangled briars and poison ivy, and steamy bogs and palmetto swamps of the Big Thicket, called by the Indians the Big Woods. The Attakapas hunted the southern fringes of the Thicket for bear, deer, and a variety of small game.

In occasional pursuit of buffalo, the Attakapas wandered southwest of their usual territory to the edges of the nearby prairies, those fabled Texas grasslands so eminently suited for grazing of livestock. However, in this direction lived the bellicose Plains Indians: the Apache, Comanche, and Tonkawa. For this reason the Attakapas generally preferred their home ground.

Never a large group, the Attakapas dwindled in number throughout the 18th century, partially because of diseases brought by the white man but perhaps also because of their inherent inability to adapt to a changing world. One by one their villages on the Neches, Trinity, and Sabine rivers were abandoned, until at some undetermined date, probably after the first quarter of the 19th century, the Attakapas disappeared completely from Southeast Texas, leaving the rich land to future colonists.

The white man first appeared on the Southeast Texas horizon in the person of a Spaniard named Alvar Nuñez Cabeza de Vaca, a member of the Pánfilo de Narváez expedition which set sail in 1528. One of many launched by the powerful Spanish Empire at the beginning of the 16th century to search for New World gold, the Narváez expedition ended when its ships were sunk in the Gulf during a hurricane.

When their ships were wrecked, Cabeza de Vaca and three other survivors were cast ashore on an island they named *Malhado*, or "Misfortune," which was probably Galveston. A mild-mannered, scholarly man who had apparently been included in the expedition as a moderating influence on the rash *conquistadores*, Cabeza de Vaca was rescued, or captured, depending upon one's point of view, by the Karankawa Indians. For eight years he survived incredible hardship, an unlikely hero, becoming a sort of medicine man to the Indians and wandering over a large

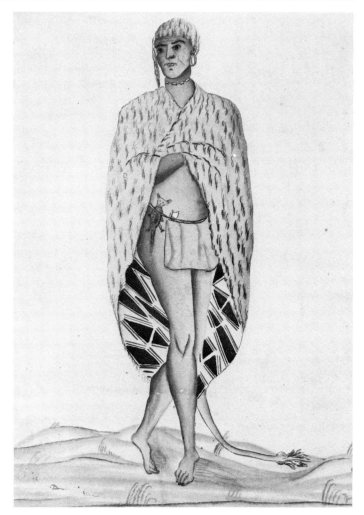

Top
Rendered circa 1732 by A. De Batz, this warrior, believed to be an Attakapas, stands tall in his favorite buffalo robe. Courtesy, Peabody Museum, Harvard University.

Above
Alvar Nuñez Cabeza de Vaca, representative of the Spanish Empire, survived shipwreck and lived among the Indians for eight years. He is shown performing surgery, presumably removing an arrow from an Indian brave. Courtesy, Texas Surgical Society.

part of Southeast Texas before eventually escaping to a Spanish outpost. Incidentally, although the Karankawa have traditionally been accused of cannibalism, Cabeza de Vaca's journal records only their horror when some of the starving Spaniards devoured their dead comrades-at-arms, fostering speculation among some historians that perhaps the Indians learned the practice from the Spaniards in the first place.

Spurred by rumors of fabulous treasure, Spain began sending more expeditions into the new territory. One such venture, first commanded by Hernando de Soto and then after his death by Luis Moscoso, explored the East Texas woods on its way from Florida overland to Mexico in 1543. Unable to reach Mexico, the members of the Moscoso expedition retraced their steps and, making crude boats, floated down the Mississippi River into the Gulf, where they were finally cast ashore near present-day Beaumont. Here they caulked their boats with the petroleum on the beaches, describing it as "a scum the sea casts up, . . . which is like pitch and is used instead on shipping, where that is not to be had."

In all, perhaps 20 Spanish expeditions ventured into the land of New Spain, as they named it, after the arrival of the first explorers. In many of their journals, these early *conquistadores* praised the natural wealth of the land. Since they failed to find gold, however, Spain gradually lost interest in the area, making no serious effort to colonize it. It remained a Spanish possession, its resources unexploited, for 150 years, its legacy from the explorers the cattle and

horses that escaped from the early expeditions to multiply on the lush blackland prairies, and the hogs that freed themselves from De Soto's entourage to become the ancestors of the piney woods razorbacks.

The primeval peace that reigned in Spanish Texas during most of the 17th century, however, was doomed to be shattered by the French. In 1684 the explorer Robert Cavelier, Sieur de la Salle, who had claimed all lands east of the Rio Grande for France, launched an expedition to settle his newly claimed territory. Aiming for the mouth of the Mississippi, he overshot his destination by some 400 miles, touching briefly at Sabine Pass before landing at Matagorda Bay. There he settled his colonists and built a wooden fort, named for the patron saint of his sovereign, King Louis XIV.

La Salle, soon realizing his error, made two treks from Fort St. Louis to find the Mississippi River. The first took him as far as the upper Trinity and Neches rivers, where he was forced to stop at a friendly Hasinai village to recover from a serious illness. The second, in 1687, ended in tragedy when La Salle, an austere, imperious man, was shot and killed by his own men somewhere in the woods of East

Above
Luis Moscoso led the De Soto expedition into East Texas and became one of the first to discover the utility of the globs of petroleum that had washed up on the beaches. He caulked his boats with the substance at Sabine Lake, southeast of Beaumont. Courtesy, Library of Congress.

Above
Just north of the bluff upon which Beaumont was born lay the Big Thicket, part a tangle of vines and underbrush, part a canopy formed by hardwoods, and part huge stands of virgin pine, laced throughout with streams. The Thicket's shadowy nature spawned more legends than did ordinary frontiers. Photo by Wesley Norton.

Texas. According to the journal of one of the men who accompanied him, the killing took place near a river, about 40 miles from the Gulf. A legend later sprang up that the river in question was the Neches and that the heinous act occurred at the Collier's Ferry crossing at the foot of the old Jasper Road, now Pine Street, in present-day Beaumont. However, historians have since placed the location of the murder near Navasota on the Brazos River.

Rumors of La Salle's incursion on Matagorda Bay abruptly jerked Spain from its complacent attitude toward its New World possessions. When an investigatory expedition, commanded by Captain Alonso de León, arrived at the site of La Salle's colony, however, they found no one. The Karankawa Indians, who had harassed the colony almost from its beginning, perhaps because of their treatment at La Salle's hands, had destroyed the settlement. The Spanish soldiers quickly burned the remnants of the fort, obliterating the last traces of that first French claim to Spanish soil.

The De León expedition then traveled to East Texas, their object to establish a mission among the powerful Hasinai confederacy, a peaceful, highly civilized group of Indians who could be depended upon to act as a deterrent to the French menace from the East. De León selected a site on the west bank of the stream the Hasinai called the Snow

River, renaming it the Neches after the Neche tribe living on its banks, and founded the mission of San Francisco de los Tejas in the year 1690, a year that also marked Spain's formal possession of Texas as a province. Thus, "tejas," the Hasinai greeting, gave Texas its name.

In the first years of the 18th century, the governor of Louisiana sent a young soldier of fortune named Louis Juchereau de St. Denis into Texas to investigate the possibility of expanding French trade with the Indians. Accordingly, St. Denis established the small settlement of Natchitoches, Louisiana, in 1713, then audaciously set out on the old *Camino Real* through the heart of Spanish Texas, suddenly appearing, to the Spaniards' astonishment, at the settlement of San Juan Bautista on the Rio Grande in July 1714.

The Spaniards, alarmed that a stranger could so easily pass through their territory, arrested St. Denis and sent him to Mexico City, where he convinced the viceroy that the French were threatening East Texas. The viceroy, taking St. Denis into Spanish pay, ordered him to reestablish the East Texas missions, which had in the interim been abandoned. In the meantime, this 18th-century double agent secretly warned the governor of Louisiana that the Spanish were reopening the missions and that the French should establish the Louisiana border at the Rio Grande.

Above
Frenchman Louis Juchereau de St. Denis came to Texas to pursue trade with the Indians. Arrested by the Spanish, he attempted to serve both Spanish mission and French trading interests. Courtesy, Sam Houston Regional Library.

Above, middle and right
French trappers and traders of the 18th century placed a special value on the furs of beaver and mink. Records of the American Fur Company show that its itinerant trappers hunted in this region. Eventually, Beaumont was to become the most important fur center west of Calcasieu Parish. Courtesy, Texas Parks and Wildlife.

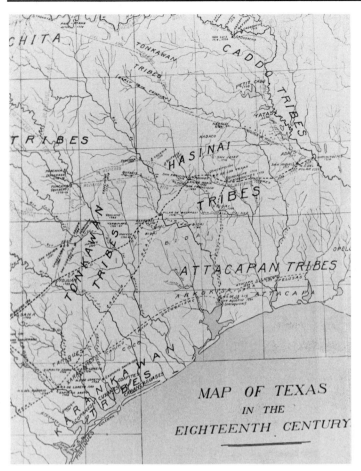

MAP OF TEXAS
IN THE
EIGHTEENTH CENTURY

In 1716 St. Denis led an *entrada* into the East Texas woods, establishing six new missions for Spain. However, his efforts were also successful from the French point of view; by 1730 French trappers and traders were crossing the Sabine River into the forbidden territory, navigating both the Neches and Trinity rivers and trading with the Indians. In 1745 a Spanish commandant at the Nabidachos village on the Neches recorded that Indians were carrying French firearms and other articles of trade such as knives, combs, mirrors, and tobacco.

As for the ebullient St. Denis, he lived in prosperity for the remainder of his life in Natchitoches with his Spanish wife, who incidentally was the granddaughter of the commandant who had arrested him at San Juan Bautista. He died in 1744 and was buried with great pomp in the Church of the Immaculate Conception at Natchitoches, which has been called the "Westminster Abbey of the French frontier." Many of his direct descendants still live in the East Texas area.

In 1754 a French trader, Joseph Blancpain, was arrested near the mouth of the Trinity River. This incident led the Spanish to establish in 1756 a mission and presidio on the Trinity called El Orcoquisac and an outpost near the modern town of Liberty, which they named *Atascosito*, or "Little Boggy." These two settlements were the Spanish communities located nearest the modern town of Beaumont. To provide access to these outposts, the Spanish carved through the prairies and timberlands a military trail that ran from Goliad to Atascosito, then turned eastward to cross the Neches at the site of present-day Beaumont. This road, known as the Atascosito Trail, or from its eastward extension the Opelousas Road, became one of the most frequently traveled routes in Texas.

The Treaty of Paris of 1763, which ended the Seven Years' War, changed the map of the entire Gulf Coast. France, as payment for help in fighting England, ceded Louisiana to Spain, while Spain was forced to give Florida to England in order to recover the island of Cuba. Spanish ownership of Louisiana obviated the necessity for the Spanish border missions in East Texas; consequently, they were again abandoned. However, a new menace to Spanish rule in Texas soon reared its head. Rumors began circulating among the Indians of English settlements near the mouth of the Neches River and of Englishmen who traveled the Trinity and the Neches, buying horses that the Indians had stolen from the Spanish.

The most serious English incursion into Southeast Texas came in 1777, when Indians of the coastal nations brought word to Antonio Gil Ybarbo, the captain of militia at the tiny Spanish pueblo of Bucareli on the Trinity River, that an English ship was stranded at the mouth of the Neches. Traveling to the coast, Ybarbo found a stranded vessel (actually in Sabine Lake) but no Englishmen, only a few huts on the riverbank not far, according to Ybarbo's crude map, from the site of present-day Beaumont. The ship contained a load of bricks in its hold. The Indians living nearby informed Ybarbo that for several years the English had been entering the Neches in small boats for trading purposes, and that in 1774 they had stayed long enough to "sow a crop," although Ybarbo could find no real settlement.

Probably used only for ballast, the bricks in the hold of the British ship nevertheless gave the suspicious Spanish

Above
A sophisticated 18th-century map of Texas locates the various Indian tribes and records Spanish activity in the region. Courtesy, Sam Houston Regional Library.

the idea that the English had come to settle. It was not the British, however, but the Anglo-Americans who constituted the ultimate threat to the New World empire of Spain. In 1783, the year the United States won recognition of its independence from England, an Indian in the service of Spain made an uncanny prophecy:

It is necessary to keep in mind that a new independent power now exists on this continent. . . . Their development will constantly menace the dominion of Spain in America and it would be an unpardonable error not to take all necessary steps to check their territorial advances by strengthening the outposts of . . . Texas, Coahuila, and New Mexico.

The dawn of the 19th century rang the death knell for Spanish occupation of Texas. Besieged on all sides, Spain was fast losing her once-mighty power, and the sun of her great New World empire was about to set. She was forced to cede Louisiana back to France in 1800. In turn, Napoleon in 1803 sold the territory to the United States, and suddenly Spanish Texas found itself bordering the upstart, burgeoning young republic to the north. To complicate matters still further, a short-lived insurrection against the Spanish government triggered a decade of discontent among Spanish Texans.

In 1818, ignoring Spanish authorities, 120 Napoleonic sympathizers came to live on the banks of the lower Trinity River, 50 miles west of present-day Beaumont, after Napo-

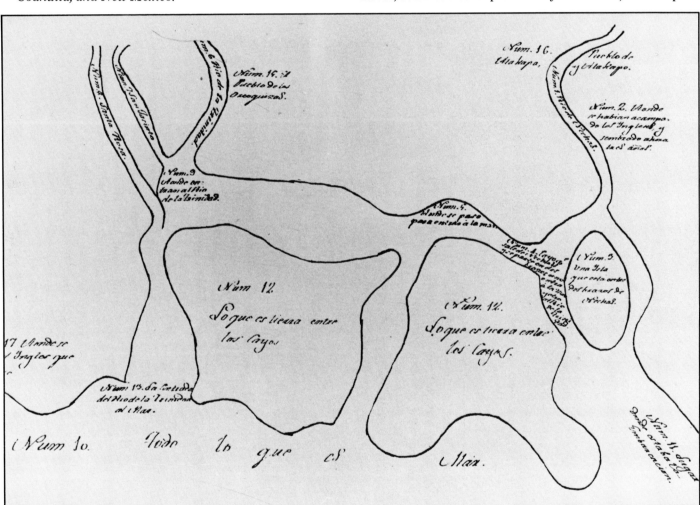

Above
A map drawn in 1777 by Captain Antonio Gil Ybarbo confirms the suspected presence of the English in Southeast Texas. The number 2 (upper right) locates the English camp along the Neches; number 11 (lower right) marks the wreckage of the English ship at Sabine Pass; number 16 (upper right) places the "Atakapa" villages on either side of the Neches. Courtesy, Texas University Publications.

leon's defeat at Waterloo. They hoped to rescue Napoleon from his captivity on St. Helena and to put his brother Joseph Bonaparte, then a resident of New Jersey, on the Mexican throne in return for aiding Mexican revolutionaries.

Named Champ d'Asile (Field of Refuge) and led by two former members of Napoleon's Imperial Guard, Generals Charles Lallemande and Antoine Rigaud, the colony on the Trinity became for a short while a *cause célèbre* among Napoleonic sympathizers in France and a source of political friction between Spain and the United States, who made simultaneous efforts to evict the colonists. In spite of its weakness, Spain sent a small military detachment to the settlement to disperse it. The soldiers found, perhaps fortunately for themselves, that Lallemande and Rigaud had

moved their colony to Galveston Island, where they soon disbanded it.

Galveston Island, in the meantime, had become a haven for Mexican revolutionaries and outlaws. Luis Michel Aury, a pirate masquerading as a Mexican patriot, established himself there in 1816. From this base Aury began harassing Spanish ships, many of which were slavers, and selling the captured slaves in Louisiana.

Aury, snug in his lair, reckoned without that consummate corsair, Jean Laffite, who arrived at Galveston Island in 1817, only days after Aury had led a revolutionary expedition down the Texas coast. By the time Aury returned from his foray, Laffite, with typical audacity, had ensconced himself in his place. Hero, traitor, man of affairs, double agent, Laffite left his indelible mark on the Gulf

---

Above
Wild geese represent the waterfowl so abundant in the marshlands in days past. They still follow the instincts of their ancestors, flying in great flocks from their breeding grounds in the north to winter in marshes and rice fields adjacent to Beaumont. Courtesy, Texas Parks and Wildlife.

Above
The tallest trees in the backwaters of the virgin forests were the stately cypress. They were the first to be commercially exploited by white settlers. Photo by Wesley Norton.

Coast area; no other man so captured the collective imaginations of southeast Texas folk as did this legendary privateer and his buccaneers.

Laffite (whose name is commonly but erroneously spelled "Lafitte") was born in 1782 in Port-au-Prince, Haiti, of French-Spanish-Jewish descent. His Jewish grandmother academically educated him; however, his practical training came from his older brother Alexander, better known as Dominique You, who initiated Jean and another brother, Pierre, into the privateering trade. The brothers, with Jean as their leader, established a base of operations on Grande Terre, an island in Barataria Bay just south of New Orleans, from which they attacked Spanish ships in the Gulf of Mexico. Laffite, handsome, cultured, and gallant, became a colorful figure on the fringes of New Orleans society, often appearing at the city's famous quadroon balls. For a time, after he aided Andrew Jackson in his victory at the Battle of New Orleans, Laffite was even regarded as a hero.

However, when he was evicted by the United States government from his commune at Barataria, Laffite's eyes turned westward toward the untapped territory of New Spain. Recruiting several hundred renegades, he established on Galveston Island his own small republic, called Campeche, which, as "bos," he ruled with an iron hand. Campeche was complete with saloons, a billiard hall, a commissary, and living quarters, and was dominated by Laffite's own residence, a combination house and fort, which he painted bright red and christened "Maison Rouge."

From Campeche, Laffite, operating under letters of marque from the Republic of Cartagena, sent his formidable fleet of privateers to prey upon Spanish slavers and merchantmen in the Gulf of Mexico, transporting the captured slaves either by boat across Sabine Lake or overland across the lower Neches and Sabine rivers to Louisiana. To accommodate his live merchandise, he built two barracoons, or slave pens, in the disputed Neutral Ground along the Sabine River: one on aptly-named Contraband Bayou and the other at Ballew's Ferry. In Louisiana, Laffite sold his slaves to his best customers, the Bowie brothers, James, Rezin, and John, who as slave dealers resold them at enormous profits.

Supposedly sympathetic to the Mexican revolutionaries, Laffite in reality sent word to his followers at Bolivar to eschew the revolution in Texas "until the right moment

and favorable time came." At the same time, he was in the secret pay of his old enemy, Spain, as has since been proved by letters in the Spanish archives. Yet the Napoleonic colonists at Champ d'Asile received his aid. Probably no one will ever know where the real sympathies of this master of duplicity lay; he remained an unfathomable enigma to all but himself.

In 1821 Laffite's luck ran out. Against his express orders one of his privateers unsuccessfully attacked an American merchantman. Pursued by the United States cutter *Lynx*, the privateer ran aground on McFaddin Beach, about 45 miles south of Beaumont. Laffite promptly hanged the offending captain, but a similar incident in 1820 brought retribution to Campeche in the person of Lieutenant Kearny of the United States brig-of-war *Enterprise*. Laffite welcomed him cordially and entertained him lavishly aboard his flagship, the *Pride*. In an account of the visit, Kearny described Laffite as a tall, dark-haired man with a mild countenance and very pleasing manners, but with a flashing "black eye" which made Kearny think that "when aroused, *Il Capitano* could be a very ugly customer indeed."

Kearny ultimately delivered his message: Laffite must leave Galveston Island. Accordingly, he dispersed his colony, sending some of his people to New Orleans and some inland along the Sabine River, thereby infusing the population of the Sabine-Neches area with the descendants of ex-privateers. In February 1821 Laffite gave the order to burn

Above
In 1818 French General Charles Lallemande landed veterans of Napoleon's defeated armies on the lower Trinity. Spain became alarmed at the news of the colony, named Champ d'Asile (Field of Refuge), and caused the settlement to be abandoned within a year. Courtesy, Spindletop Museum.

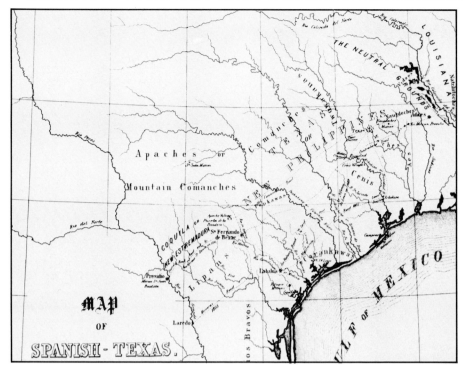

Campeche to the ground. He described the scene in his journal:

Everyone left the island at four o'clock. Then the sky brightened and a breeze came from the northwest. Homes were put to the torch and blazed all along the shore. My ships headed toward the south. Four leagues out at sea I could still see Galveston on fire, looking like a sunset. That was the last time I saw the Gulf of Texas . . .

A flamboyant figure in life, Laffite the man was nevertheless eclipsed shortly after his departure from Galveston by Laffite the legend. Within a few years of his sailing, the entire Gulf Coast was rife with fantastic tales of the treasure he had supposedly buried in every bayou, inlet, or shellbank from New Orleans to Matagorda, each site guarded by its own resident ghost. Over the years treasure hunters employed "authentic" maps, divining rods, and other devices in a fruitless search for pirate gold. The descendants of Joseph Pivoto, an early area settler who was rumored to have been linked with Laffite, saw as recently as the 1950s freshly dug holes in the yard behind the Pivoto

homestead, testimony to an enduring legend. Laffite himself said, regarding his booty:

Stories have been circulated . . . that I have hidden silver and gold on the sandy islands all along the Gulf Coast . . . It is true. There are things hidden here and there, but I haven't the slightest idea of the exact spots, nor would I wish to waste time trying to recover lost valuables or buried treasure.

I do have some things of value near New Orleans, buried in a small estuary under shelter. They are safe and the location is known by no one in the world except me.

After leaving Galveston, Laffite lived in hiding while he spread conflicting tales of his own demise; in fact, most accounts of his life end with his supposed death in 1826. His journal states, however, that on New Year's Day 1826, he and his brother Pierre, in what is surely one of the most monumental New Year's resolutions ever made, decided to "give up the cause," terminating their so-called business affairs and dividing up their property. Laffite then moved to

Above
An early 19th-century map of Spanish Texas identifies the "neutral grounds" which were established between Spanish Texas and French Louisiana. Courtesy, Barker History Collection.

Above
Jane Wilkinson Long was the niece of General James Wilkinson, who received the transfer of Louisiana from France to the United States and later figured in the treason trial of Aaron Burr. Mrs. Long became known as "The Mother of Texas." Living alone on Bolivar Peninsula except for her two-year-

old daughter and a slave girl named Kiamatia, she gave birth during the winter of 1821 to the first Anglo child born in Texas, delivering it herself. Her husband, Dr. James Long, was killed for his rebellion against Spanish rule. Courtesy, Southwestern Collection.

the eastern United States, living out the rest of his life in comfortable obscurity under the assumed name of John Lafflin. He died in 1854 in Alton, Illinois.

While Laffite still ruled Galveston, Dr. James Long, a Natchez physician whose purpose was to free Texas from Spanish rule, led a filibustering expedition into Texas in 1819. A persuasive, charismatic man who was also impulsive and short-sighted, Long approached Laffite with the hope of inducing him to help his cause. Laffite paid lip service to Long but privately warned his own men at Bolivar to remain independent of Long's venture.

From Bolivar peninsula, across the bay from Galveston, Long and his men embarked for Mexico, leaving his pregnant wife Jane, their two-year-old baby, and a slave alone on the narrow spit of land. After an incredibly harsh

winter during which Jane Long was forced to deliver her own baby, who incidentally was the first Anglo-American infant to be born in Texas, the little party was rescued by a fellow immigrant. Shortly thereafter Mrs. Long received word of her husband's assassination in Mexico City.

Although Long's expedition failed, dissatisfaction with the Spanish government continued to grow in the territory of Texas. As the long twilight of Spanish rule in the New World drew toward its inevitable close, there remained only three Spanish settlements of any consequence in the entire province of Texas: San Antonio, La Bahía (Goliad), and Nacogdoches. Probably to the relief of all concerned, a bloodless revolution in 1821 established the independence of Mexico, setting the stage for the Anglo-American era in Texas and for the settlement of the town of Beaumont.

Above
Jean Laffite cuts a dashing figure as a pirate, at least in the imagination of the artist. Colonial rivalries and general political instability along the Gulf Coast encouraged the presence of an assortment of pirates, filibusterers, and revolutionaries. Courtesy, Spindletop Museum.

Above
Perhaps Laffite had retired from piracy by the time he was captured by the realism of the camera. Pirate or not, Laffite looks thoroughly domesticated as he poses with his second wife. Courtesy, Sam Houston Regional Library.

Chapter II

The Town and the Republic

We are informed that a town has lately been laid out on the tidewater of the river Neches, at a place known as Tevis Bluff, 30 miles from Sabine Bay. Its situation is said to be one of the most delightful in Texas and it has already commenced improving at a rapid rate. It is spoken of as a town which promises to be one of considerable importance. It has received the name of Beaumont, *which, from the description of the place, strikes our fancy as very appropriate.*

—Telegraph and Texas Register,
San Felipe de Austin, October 26, 1835

Sam Houston, the military champion of San Jacinto, became the Republic's first president and a firm supporter of Texas' admission to the Union. He lost favor among the people of his state when he refused to endorse secession. Courtesy, Business Men's Studio.

While Mexico was winning its independence from Spain, a new spirit of expansion was making itself felt in the young republic to the north, which would profoundly and permanently affect the future of Texas. Americans, looking westward, realized that they could utilize the vast unclaimed lands of their young nation to extend their boundaries—and horizons—to the limits of their imaginations. Impelled by the force of that idea, Americans swarmed into the western territories, in time casting greedy eyes on the fertile lands of Mexican Texas. In 1821 a 27-year-old Missourian named Stephen Fuller Austin secured permission from the Mexican government to settle a colony of Anglo-Americans along the Brazos, Colorado, and Bernard rivers. In fulfillment of the Indian's prophecy, Anglo-American Texas was about to become a reality.

Hard upon the heels of Austin's Old Three Hundred, as his original colonists came to be known, followed crowds of other Anglo-American settlers pouring into Texas under the liberal colonization laws of the Mexican government. Most settled in the interior of the state under the auspices of an *empresario* because of Mexico's ban on colonization within 20 leagues (60 miles) of its borders, but a few defied the law and independently made their homes along the lower reaches of the Trinity and Neches rivers. Among these latter settlers were Noah and Nancy Tevis.

In moving to Texas, Noah Tevis, a Scotsman born in Maryland in 1782, followed a migration pattern typical of many Anglo-Americans who came to the new territory. He left Maryland for Tennessee, then moved to Louisiana, where he married Nancy Nixon, a lady of French descent 13 years his junior, and fathered seven children. From Louisiana, the Tevises traveled westward by covered wagon on the Opelousas Trail, crossing the Sabine River into Texas sometime in 1824. Their journey came to an end on a thickly wooded bluff on the west bank of the Neches a short distance from the Opelousas Trail crossing, where they built a modest two-room log cabin with a mud chimney. Tevis cleared a 20-acre field, put in a subsistence crop, probably of corn and sweet potatoes, and planted peach and fig trees near his house. He built a cattle pen and began raising stock, either with animals he had brought with him or with wild cattle caught on the nearby prairies. Here Nancy Tevis gave birth to their eighth child, probably the first white baby born in the Sabine-Neches area. The Tevis farm and the little community that later grew up around it became known as Tevis Bluff, or the Neches River Settlement.

Although for several years the Tevises lived alone on the Neches, other immigrants soon began moving into the Trinity-Neches area. Eventually the colonists along the two rivers organized themselves into the Municipality of Atascocito, after the old Spanish settlement on the Trinity River. It comprised the area now including the present-day counties of Liberty, Chambers, Jefferson, Orange, San Jacinto, Polk, Tyler, Hardin, Jasper, and Newton. It remained a loosely self-governed entity until 1831, when it became the Municipality of Liberty and was absorbed into the Department of Nacogdoches.

In 1829, Mexico, relaxing its ban on border colonization, gave the settlement of the territory immediately west of the Sabine River into the hands of Mexican native Lorenzo de Zavala, *empresario*, scholar and statesman, who from his base in Nacogdoches began issuing land titles in the area of present-day Jefferson County.

Above right
This drawing of the cabin of Noah and Nancy Tevis is based upon a detailed description by Joseph Pulsifer. The floors were made of earth, the door was of dried cowhide, the roof was of split boards held by weight poles, and there was a typical dog-trot between the rooms. The Tevis family grew an assortment of fruit in their yard. Drawing by Roma Ornelas.

Right
Lorenzo de Zavala received an impresario grant from the Mexican government in 1827. One of the signers of the Texas Declaration of Independence, he later served as interim vice-president of the Republic of Texas.

In 1834 Noah Tevis formally applied to De Zavala's land office in Nacogdoches for ownership of the land he had been farming without benefit of authority:

Mr. Special Commissioner of the Colony of Mr. Lorenzo de Zavala; Noah Tevis, a native of the United States of the North, with due respect comes before you and says: having been attracted by the generous disposition of the (government) of the laws of the State I have come with my family, consisting of my wife and seven children, to settle in this colony; that on seeing the certificate accompanying this you will be kind enough to admit me as a settler in the aforesaid colony. Grant me the quantity of land that I may be entitled to in the vacant lands of the same. For this to you I pray that you may act as I ask that I may receive grace and justice. Nacogdoches, Dec. 13, 1834.

Tevis received half a league of land, or approximately 2,214 acres, on "the western margin of the River Neches" in January 1835. The grant was signed by George Antonio Nixon, the land commissioner for De Zavala's office.

In the meantime, several families had joined the Tevises on or near the bluff on the Neches River. Thomas F. and Joshua Lewis immigrated to Texas and Tevis Bluff in 1830, building two cabins there, and a Danish immigrant, Christian Hillebrandt, came to live a few miles south of the settlement in 1831. Joseph Grigsby trekked in 1834 to a spot on the Neches a few miles downriver from the community, where he established a cotton plantation, complete with several slaves.

The Ashworth family, Aaron, Abner, William, and Jesse, came to live east of the Neches between 1831-1834. A swarthy clan, they were thought by their contemporaries to be mulattoes, and were listed as such on the census. There is considerable doubt, however, that they were of black origin, as their features were apparently Caucasian. Thomas Jefferson Russell, writing in 1910, suggested that they were of Portuguese Moorish descent, and Ashworth family research has indicated that they were of French and English extraction.

Whatever their origins, the Ashworths grew to be among the wealthiest ranchers and slaveholders in the area. When the Congress of the Republic of Texas passed a law prohibiting free "persons of color" from living in Texas, the Ashworths were powerful enough to secure an amendment, afterward called the "Ashworth law," that allowed them to remain in Texas because they had been residents there at the signing of the Texas declaration of independence. However, tensions resulting from the execution in 1856 of Jack Bunch, a cousin of the Ashworths and the convicted murderer of a deputy sheriff, caused most of the family to leave the area shortly thereafter.

In 1833 James and Elizabeth McFaddin, who had first settled in 1823 at Moss Bluff, below Liberty, moved to Tevis Bluff and built a cabin on land immediately north of Noah Tevis on the Neches River. From this modest beginning sprang a dynasty of strong individuals who would have a profound influence on the future of cattle ranching in the area.

Above
When building their cabins, East Texas settlers squared the logs on four sides and joined the corners as shown. Clay lined the fireplace, and sticks, moss, and mud furnished all but the workmanship for the "mud cat" chimney. Photo by Wesley Norton. Courtesy, Spindletop Museum.

Above right
William McFaddin moved to Beaumont in 1833 with his parents, James and Elizabeth, and married Rachael Williams in 1837. He led the McFaddin family to dominance in land and cattle in the Beaumont area. Courtesy, Tyrrell Historical Library.

Facing page
Top
Henry Stephenson, the founder of Methodism in Texas, visited the Beaumont area in 1834, returning in 1840 to conduct a brush arbor revival. This compass, now minus its needle, guided him through the wilderness of East Texas. Photo by Wesley Norton. Courtesy, First Methodist Church.

Bottom
Henry Millard and George Patillo of the Beaumont Board of Aldermen denied a grant of land to Joseph Yates "on account of his color" even before the Texas Legislature passed an Exclusion Act in 1840. Courtesy, Sam Houston Regional Library.

While others were searching for good farmlands on which to settle, one man was exploring a different aspect of the land. Kentuckian Dr. John Allen Veatch, physician, botanist, geologist, and surveyor who had immigrated to Nacogdoches in 1833, became intrigued with the mineralogy of the region while surveying for the Mexican government. Receiving land as a fee for his services, he chose it in separate parcels, one including the low hill south of Tevis Bluff and its nearby sour springs, containing mineral waters and varicolored muds credited by the Indians with medicinal powers. The other parcel included a similar spot north of town, near present-day Sour Lake. Contemporary sources report not only that Veatch spoke of creating health spas at both locations, but also that he was aware of the great pool of crude oil floating in the Gulf of Mexico just west of Sabine Pass which disappeared in 1902, a year after the discovery of the Spindletop oil field.

A man of restless disposition, Veatch moved to California in the wake of the Gold Rush, subsequently discovering the extensive borax deposits in Lake County before finally moving to Portland, Oregon, where he died in 1870. Even though he never utilized his land in Texas, it is significant that he deliberately chose land containing two piercement salt domes as his headright, thereby foreshadowing the discovery of oil in both locations half a century later.

The year 1835 saw the arrival of two men who would be leading citizens of the future town of Beaumont: Henry Millard and Joseph Pulsifer. Millard, a merchant first in Natchez and then in New Orleans, was to emerge for a time not only as the dominant figure in the small community on the Neches, but also as a Texas statesman and military leader. Pulsifer, a perceptive, literate man originally from Massachusetts, was to serve as the town's apothecary, first postmaster, and one of its leading businessmen until his death in 1867. He never married, legend having it that he tragically lost his fiancée, Joseph Grigsby's daughter Margaret, to illness a short time before their intended marriage.

According to an account by Pulsifer, the two men formed a partnership in New Orleans with a third party, Thomas B. Huling, the object being to establish the mercantile business in Southeast Texas. On July 10, 1835, Huling and Pulsifer sailed from New Orleans on the schooner *Commercial*, which took them as far as Sabine Lake before grounding in its muddy shallows. After hiring a "lighter," or small boat, to carry them over the shallow bar at the mouth of the Neches, they landed just south of Tevis Bluff at Santa Anna, a tiny community which had been named in an excess of premature zeal for General Antonio Lopez de Santa Anna, the head of the Mexican government.

Pulsifer and Huling began moving their goods up to their store at Santa Anna, which included not only such stock items as tools, powder, guns, glassware, salt, bagging, baling, and rope, but such esoterica as Bateman's Drops, Carpenter's Sarsaparilla, opium, Balsam of Life, corrosive sublimate, and lunar caustic, undoubtedly tools of Pulsifer's profession. Pulsifer had located the store:

50 rods up the river from the landing on quite high ground perhaps twenty-five foot from the surface of the river. It is placed in the midst of the forest perhaps 150 feet from the bank of the river, trees of every description, pines, oak, ash, and hickory growing round so thick that not more than 600 rods could be seen any way from it excepting toward the river where the view could extend to the other side.

After Pulsifer and Huling finished stocking the store, they were given a guided tour of "town" by Joseph Grigsby, whom Pulsifer described as "a patriarchal old gentleman with whom I had much pleasant conversation relative to the manners and customs of the Texians." Following a footpath through the dense woods, Pulsifer, Huling, and Grigsby passed a small log house used as a school, and a store owned by Captain Samuel Rodgers, a land promoter and the Mexican customs official at Santa Anna. Continuing

Above
The first marriage in Beaumont, that of Mary Tevis to Gilbert Stephenson, was officially performed "in bond" due to the absence of a priest. In spite of the legal inconvenience it was an elaborate social event. From Stratton, History of Beaumont.

north along the riverbank, they paid a visit to Noah Tevis, who lived half a mile beyond the Rodgers store. Pulsifer described Tevis as "a most singular being" who set out "spirit and cups" and served them a snack of ripe figs for their refreshment. After sitting for a time with Mr. Tevis in his open hallway, or "dog-trot," they proceeded through the woods to visit several more families in the little settlement, which, Pulsifer declared, "consisted of but twelve homes and ninety individuals great and small." He quickly adapted to his new surroundings, building a "capacious log home placed in the midst of a forest bordering a view . . . than which there can be no more beautiful in the world."

Small as they were, the two tiny communities of Tevis Bluff and Santa Anna obviously showed potential to enterprising minds. In the fall of 1835, Henry Millard, who had also arrived in the area the previous July, purchased 50 acres of the Noah Tevis survey and with his partners Huling and Pulsifer laid out the town of Beaumont, in the process giving it a new title, for it had outgrown both its names.

There are many stories of how Beaumont received its name; however, the most credible tale states that Henry Millard, the unquestioned leader of the colony, named the town for his recently deceased wife, Natchez belle Mary Dewburleigh Barlace Warren Beaumont. Supporting this theory is the fact that one of Henry Millard's sons was named Henry Beaumont Millard. Another story holds that Millard, who was a delegate to the Consultation of 1835 and was instrumental in forming the new Municipality of Jefferson (present-day Orange County), named both the town and the new county for his wife's brother, Thomas Jefferson Beaumont. It is possible that Millard chose the name of a revered American President because it was also the name of his brother-in-law; the story, however, although supported by Millard family tradition, lacks documentation.

All plans for development of the new town were abruptly halted by the oncoming Texas Revolution. Even though Anglo-American colonists in Texas considered themselves to be citizens of the Republic of Mexico, distance from the seat of government and diversity of culture and religion had created a potentially unstable situation, which was exacerbated by the assumption of the dictatorship of Mexico by General Santa Anna, the self-styled "Napoleon of the West."

At first loyal to Santa Anna, the Texians refused to entertain the idea of revolution. However, as he became

more and more dictatorial, they became increasingly opposed to his policies. Anahuac, where in January 1835 Santa Anna had sent a small detachment of troops to enforce customs collections, was the scene of the first hostilities. There Colonel William Barret Travis captured the Mexican garrison and took 44 prisoners. After Anahuac, most of the colonists were willing to fight, but still believed themselves to be fighting for their rights under the Mexican Constitution of 1824 rather than for their independence. Pulsifer wrote from Beaumont in 1835:

Texas . . . at that time alone stood out against Santa Anna with his mighty power. . . . [Texians] dared to make a stand for their freedom, to never live under a government less liberal than the constitution of Mexico . . . .

Above
Antonio Lopez de Santa Anna, the "Napoleon of the West," suffered humiliating defeat by Sam Houston's Texian Army at the Battle of San Jacinto on April 21, 1836. Houston, the victor and new hero of Texas, graciously spared Santa Anna's life.

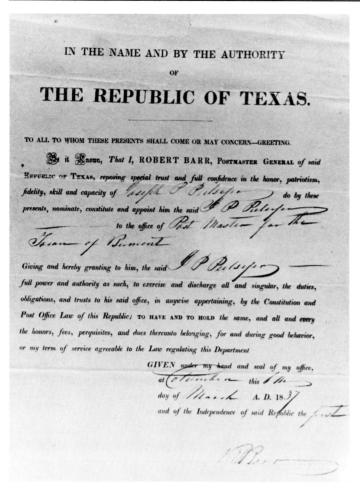

IN THE NAME AND BY THE AUTHORITY

OF

THE REPUBLIC OF TEXAS.

TO ALL TO WHOM THESE PRESENTS SHALL COME OR MAY CONCERN—GREETING.

Be it Known, That I, ROBERT BARR, POSTMASTER GENERAL of said Republic of Texas, reposing special trust and full confidence in the honor, patriotism, fidelity, skill and capacity of *Joseph P. Pulsifer* do by these presents, nominate, constitute and appoint him the said *J. P. Pulsifer* to the office of *Post Master for the Town of Beaumont*

Giving and hereby granting to him, the said *J P Pulsifer* full power and authority as such, to exercise and discharge all and singular, the duties, obligations, and trusts to his said office, in anywise appertaining, by the Constitution and Post Office Law of this Republic; TO HAVE AND TO HOLD the same, and all and every the honors, fees, perquisites, and dues thereunto belonging, for and during good behavior, or my term of service agreeable to the Law regulating this Department

GIVEN under my hand and seal of my office, at *Columbia* this *1th* day of *March* A. D. 18*37* and of the Independence of said Republic the *first*

Pulsifer also reported that on July 26, 1835, he met with his fellow townspeople at Samuel Rodgers' store to "elect officers and form a military company." In September word came that General Martín Perfecto de Cós was bringing troops to Texas with the object of subduing its rebellious inhabitants; as a consequence, Henry Millard addressed a meeting of the citizens of Beaumont at which those present favored calling a state convention. After that meeting Major Millard, as he was now styled, began on Sundays to drill the military company. He also drafted a set of resolutions, which included naming their voluntary corps the "Neches Guards" (their motto: "Try us"), and appointing a committee of correspondence, composed of himself, Burrell Eaves, and Pulsifer.

On October 10 the company again gathered, this time to choose Henry Millard as their delegate to the Consultation

at San Felipe, to be held that November. Since by then the Mexican army was threatening Texas in earnest, the Beaumont conclave, instead of holding a lengthy meeting, sent a group of men to join the Texian army.

Millard, who as leader of the Beaumont military company had traveled with them as far as San Antonio, returned to San Felipe around the first of November to attend the Consultation, which, while establishing a provisional government for the Mexican state of Texas, still stopped short of declaring independence from Mexico. However, it provided for the formation of an army, appointing Sam Houston as commander-in-chief. Millard, receiving the commission of Lieutenant Colonel of the First Regiment of Texas Infantry, departed for Nacogdoches, where he was stationed as a recruiting officer.

Pulsifer remained in Beaumont, one of only four or five men there, tending the store, serving as the secretary of the committee of safety and correspondence, and in the meantime being made Beaumont's first postmaster. He noted the death on December 6 of Noah Tevis. At midnight on Christmas Eve Pulsifer was awakened by the gunfire, shouts, and laughter of the men who brought the news of the victory at San Antonio de Bexar. Several Beaumonters had been among the 300 Texian volunteers who had followed "Old Ben Milam" into San Antonio, including 16-year-old William McFaddin. A ball was held in Beaumont January 1, 1836, to celebrate the victory.

The triumph was shortlived, however, for in the early spring of 1836 the Mexican army again took San Antonio, trapping 180 Texian troops in the Alamo, an abandoned Spanish mission. On March 1 Joseph Dunman, an army courier, galloped into Liberty, bearing Colonel William Barret Travis's last appeal for help from the Alamo. As the word spread throughout the district, Beaumonters responded by sending 28 men to join the Third Company Infantry, Second Regiment, Texas Volunteers, led by Captain William M. Logan. The company set off to join the Texian army, only to be met on the road near San Felipe with the news of the fall of the Alamo and the deaths of the Texians defending it.

In the meantime, more and more Texians were coming to believe that their only recourse was to declare complete independence from Mexico. Millard, a moderate who originally had been a strong supporter of the Mexican constitution, was won over to belief in independence late in 1835, articulating his feelings in a letter from Nacogdoches to

Above
Joseph Pulsifer was the first postmaster in Beaumont, receiving his appointment in March of 1837 from Robert Barr, Postmaster General of the Republic of Texas. Courtesy, Zulieka Elizabeth Winslow Semans.

Joseph Pulsifer:

I hope I have done with politics except to fight for independence; as for the mere shadow of a ghost called the Constitution of 1824, I'll none of it nor will any man in the present army. Texas must declare for independence or put in jeopardy her political freedom.

The Texian convention, held at the new town of Washington-on-the-Brazos in March 1836, recognized the inevitable by drafting a declaration of independence, writing a constitution, electing officers, and assuming the government of the soon-to-be Republic of Texas. In spite of the convention's determined activities, however, the outlook for the Texian army was grim. In addition to the shortage of arms, ammunition, and provisions, the defeat at the Alamo and, soon after, the massacre of Colonel James W. Fannin and 350 Texians at Goliad had dangerously lowered morale.

As Sam Houston and the Texian army began a long retreat eastward, word flew before them that the Texians were defeated and that Santa Anna, at the head of thousands of Mexican troops, was in close pursuit. Total panic ensued among the settlers, triggering what has become known as the Runaway Scrape. Families instantly left their houses and lands, sometimes literally in the middle of a meal, traveling by horse, in ox-drawn wagon, or on foot toward the Sabine River, the United States, and safety. As the crowds moving eastward grew larger and the heavy April rains came, the roads, never in good condition, became rivers of mud, slowing progress almost to a standstill. Families began discarding goods, leaving clothes, mattresses, furniture, and other belongings by the sides of the roads. Children fell unnoticed from the wagons, to be picked up and cared for by those in wagons behind them, but often to remain separated from their frantic families for weeks. To complicate the situation, the rains had greatly swollen the rivers, making the Trinity, Neches, and Sabine virtually impassable.

Refugees poured into Beaumont but, unable to cross the Neches, camped for weeks on its banks. Some went south to Grigsby's Bluff, where they traveled by boat across Sabine Lake to Louisiana. Nancy Tevis, who with the help of her children and two slaves had continued to work her land after her husband's death, chose to stay at home rather than flee, giving the refugees such help as she was able. Two new rumors were added to the tales of Mexican invasion from the west: one that the Mexican army had taken Nacogdoches and was actually advancing south between the Neches and the Sabine rivers, and the other that hostile Indians were preparing an attack on Beaumont. Pulsifer, laboring alone in his store to pack his goods with moss, declared that the reports were "so frightful ... that I expected nothing more than to see the brown or red forms of the Mexicans and Indians peering at me through the woods."

As a result of these new threats, total chaos ensued; not knowing which direction to go, people began milling about in despair. Some of the settlers attempted to fortify Grigsby's Bluff with cotton bales and a "swivel," or small

Above
George W. Smyth of Jasper County, signer of the Texas Declaration of Independence, eventually held office as the first congressman from the district which included Beaumont. Courtesy, Tyrrell Historical Library.

cannon, and station every man there, armed, while the families were removed. Pulsifer, paddling down the Neches to Grigsby's Bluff in a canoe, described the scene:

For a great distance the ground was completely spotted with people lying a-sleeping and this great number notwithstanding a sloop and a large scow had the day before carried as many families from there as they could. They were taking them all to a cockle shell bluff on the American side of the Sabine.

Meanwhile, Houston, continuing his retreat, finally halted his army at Harrisburg on the banks of the San Jacinto River, (or the "Sank-in-Sink," as Pulsifer called it), where on April 21, 1836, during the Mexican siesta hour, he engaged and defeated Santa Anna in a decisive 18-minute battle. Henry Millard distinguished himself at San Jacinto, leading four companies of infantry in the charge on the Mexican camp, and bringing home from the scene of surrender a pair of Santa Anna's pistols. For his valor, Millard gained the lasting friendship of General Sam Houston. Several area men who were in Logan's company participated in the battle, among them David McFaddin, M.J. Brake (whose musket broke during the fray), Benjamin F. Harper, Michel Pivoto, and Hezekiah Williams. William McFaddin missed the action because his company was

guarding a baggage train three miles away.

Beaumonters and refugees alike were jubilant at news of the victory at San Jacinto. Pulsifer perhaps spoke for everyone when he wrote his sister: "O Lucy how my heart did jump for joy to hear this most glad tidings; how grateful I felt for the relation of them."

As the last weary vagabonds joyfully if perhaps somewhat sheepishly began to return to their homes, and the soldiers late of the Texian army straggled back to Beaumont, the citizens of the little Neches River village again faced the

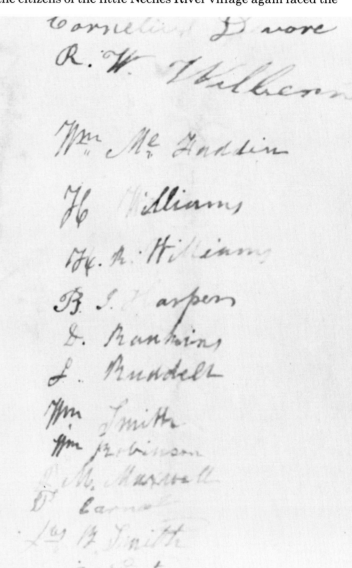

Above
A handbill dated two days after the Battle of San Jacinto, but not anticipating the outcome, shows the desperation of Texas leaders, who promised an excellent deal in land for those willing to take the risk of becoming Texians. Courtesy, Sam Houston Regional Library.

Above
This muster roll, dated May 10, 1836, two and a half weeks after the Battle of San Jacinto, was signed by each man to certify his claim to cash and spoils. William McFaddin, David McFaddin, John Stephenson, Michel Pivoto, and Hezekiah Williams were among Beaumonters on this roll. Courtesy, Sam Houston Regional Library.

tasks at which they had been interrupted when the war began: clearing land, planting crops, building houses, electing leaders, and above all, developing their town.

In September 1836, Beaumonters helped to elect as the first president of the infant Republic of Texas, General Sam Houston, the hero of the Battle of San Jacinto and an overwhelming popular favorite (forty-three Beaumonters voted for Houston, two for Stephen F. Austin). Upon assuming office, Houston appointed first Nathan Halbert, then Chichester Chaplain as chief justice of the Municipality of Jefferson. Following Chaplain's resignation in November 1837, the Old Chief appointed his friend Henry Millard to take Chaplain's place.

In the meantime, Millard, an energetic man, had returned his attentions to the project he had laid aside when he had gone to war: the townsite of Beaumont. Using as a basis the original 50 acres, already known by the name of Beaumont, that he had purchased from Noah Tevis in 1835, Millard formed a real-estate company with Pulsifer and Huling, which added 50 more acres to the site. The company then included in the partnership Nancy Tevis and Joseph Grigsby, who each contributed 50 acres, making a total of 200 acres on the high ground along the Neches River. The agreement, dated July 12, 1837, stated that the partners "have this day entered into mutual agreement for the enlargement and more perfect formation of the town."

In December 1837, the First Congress of the Republic of Texas established the county system, extending the boundaries of the existing Municipality of Jefferson to the west to include Beaumont, which prior to that date had been a part of the Municipality of Liberty. Henry Millard then exercised his influence to have the county seat of the new Jefferson County changed from the old location at Cow Bayou, or Jefferson, to Beaumont, by January 1, 1838.

Above
Henry Millard, pictured here, joined Joseph Pulsifer, Thomas Huling, Nancy Tevis, and Joseph Grigsby in laying out the village of Beaumont. Courtesy, Mary Clare Pye Wilsford.

The new county seat of Beaumont was finally incorporated as a town on December 16, 1838, by an act of the Third Congress of the Republic of Texas, the incorporation act being signed by President Mirabeau Bonaparte Lamar. On August 8, 1840, the town's first elected officials were sworn into office. Elected mayor was Alexander Calder, a New Yorker who had traveled to Beaumont by horseback in 1838 and had become a lawyer after his arrival. H.B. Littlefield was elected secretary, and Henry Millard, Charles D. Swaine, and I.F. Clark were elected aldermen. The new mayor promptly addressed himself to the problems at hand, appointing committees in charge of roads and streets, finances and accounts, landings, wharves and ferries, and, to make sure all miscellaneous ground was covered, "general expediencies."

During this postwar time, one of the first concerns of both the city government and the Jefferson County Board of Commissioners was the construction and maintenance of roads. By 1840, four roads met in Beaumont, one going east by Ballew's Ferry to Louisiana, one south to Grigsby's Bluff, one north to Woodville and Town Bluff, and one, the old Atascocito Trail, to Liberty. The board of commissioners directed new roads to be cut, in one instance ordering a 60-foot-wide road to be constructed from the "northwest rim of Main Street" to Village Creek. Beaumont's citizens, among them members of the McFaddin family, joined in clearing Main Street of trees and brush. Appointees of the county called "reviewers of roads" kept the existing roads under surveillance, drafting citizens to repair them if repair was needed.

In the absence of bridges, ferries were of vital importance in traversing the network of rivers and bayous. Beaumont in its early days had several ferries. Collier's Ferry, dating from 1831, which Henry Millard had operated at one time, was located on the Neches five miles north of Beaumont. Downriver, ferries were run at Grigsby's Bluff and Smith's Bluff. From the 1820s Noah and Nancy Tevis had operated a ferry on the Neches at the old Opelousas Trail crossing near their homestead which, after Noah's death, Nancy continued to run, building extra cow-pens for live-stock and training two or three of her cattle to lead the herds across the river on their way to the Louisiana market. She charged three cents a head for cattle, 25 cents a wheel for carts and carriages, 25 cents for a man and horse, and $6 "for a wagon and team, and all persons belonging to the same." Since ferries were not only a thriving business but also a vital cog in the public machinery, the city government kept a regulatory eye on them; one of the first ordinances passed by the new city council established liability for removing carcasses of cattle that had drowned while they were being driven across the Neches.

Although roads and ferries were important to transportation in the early days of Beaumont, they were still extremely primitive; the fastest and most efficient travel during this era was still via the waterways. The Neches and its tributary, the Angelina, provided access from the East Texas settlements down to Beaumont and thence to Sabine Pass by flatboat and keelboat. Downriver, scows, sloops, and shallow-draft sailing vessels plying their way up and down the Neches linked Beaumont to the rest of the world through Sabine Pass, Galveston, and New Orleans.

Above
Thomas F. McKinney, a resident in Austin's colony, received the first grant in what is now Jefferson County. In 1830 he operated a keelboat on the Neches River, eventually carrying cotton to New Orleans. Courtesy, William T. Block.

Even waterways such as the Neches, however, had severe drawbacks. The river itself was treacherous; shifting masses of silt and underwater snags made its navigation extremely hazardous. Moreover, the shallow bars at its mouth and at the mouth of Sabine Lake not only prevented large ships from sailing upriver, but also handicapped flatboats and keelboats moving downriver from East Texas, forcing them to depend upon seasonal high water levels and rapid currents to reach Sabine Pass and the ocean-going schooners waiting there for their cargoes. In 1843 Dr. Stephen H. Everett, Jefferson County's senator to the First Congress of the Republic of Texas, wrote its president, Anson Jones:

There must be some place for the receiving and forwarding of the cotton of Texas at the mouths of the Neches and Sabine. The Sabine Pass is not suitable, because flat boats coming down the river cannot cross the lake [Sabine Lake] with safety and that, and keel boats, are the only kinds of boats that can at this time come down the river Neches, and it will require much labor before steamboats can navigate the river.

Above
In this petition, written in Henry Millard's hand and dated October 18, 1839, the founders of Beaumont asked the Congress of the Republic of Texas to repeal the original Act of Incorporation and substitute one more to their liking. There is no indication that the petition moved the Congress. Courtesy, Mary Clare Pye Wilsford.

The possibility that the "some place" so desired by Dr. Everett might be Beaumont first occurred to its citizens in the mid-1840s, when, against all probability, a large ocean-going schooner somehow made its way up the Neches to Beaumont. Its captain took a sounding in the center of the river, discovering, to everyone's astonishment, that the depth of the river at the end of the Pearl Street dock was over 60 feet. This knowledge undoubtedly set minds to work on the idea of clearing the downriver bars and log jams to allow large ships to sail directly into Beaumont. As Everett had pointed out, much labor would indeed be required, but the idea of Beaumont as a major deepwater port, once implanted, would prove in the future to be a productive one.

By whatever means of transportation available, settlers continued to move into the fledgling town, among them people who provided badly needed professional services. Beaumont acquired its first physician in the person of Henry Millard's brother, Dr. Darcourt Josiah Otho Millard, a doctor and apothecary. (In 1841 Henry Millard had sold his interest in his store to his brother Sidney and

his brother-in-law, George Bryan, and moved to Galveston, presumably to seek new business opportunities, where he died in 1844.) D.J.O. Millard followed his brother Henry in office as chief justice of Jefferson County in 1841, and in May 1846 assumed proprietorship of the Millard family store. Frederick W. Ogden, who came from his native state of Kentucky to Beaumont in 1838, was the town's first lawyer, though he was trained in both law and medicine; from 1839 to 1842 he was the district attorney for the Fifth Judicial District of Texas and was a representative to the Seventh and Eighth Congresses of the Republic of Texas.

In 1838 Simon Wiess, a native of Poland who had become a Nacogdoches storekeeper, began a grocery store on Main Street. He moved in the same year to a site some miles up the Neches River, afterward known as Wiess Bluff, but his sons remained in Beaumont as successful businessmen. A Pennsylvanian named Isaiah Junker set up his blacksmith shop on the east side of the Jasper Road, eventually serving Beaumont well, not only as its blacksmith but also as legislator, chief justice of Jefferson County, railroad promoter, and finally as merchant.

Above
James Biddle Langham began farming in Jefferson County in 1836 and opened a livery stable in Beaumont in 1879. In 1860 he owned property valued at $25,000. Courtesy, William T. Block.

Above
Eddie H. McCain, shown here during the 1981 Spindletop Boom Days, shaped a horseshoe from a piece of metal rod, following exactly the same procedure used by Isaiah Junker during his years as Beaumont's only blacksmith. Photo by Wesley Norton.

Naturally enough, however, the occupations of most of the earliest Beaumonters were related to the land. By the time of the Republic, small sugar cane plantations, with horse- or mule-driven mills, had begun to appear. Cotton was grown in a moderate amount, principally by Joseph Grigsby and J. Biddle Langham. Langham, a Tennessean who came to Texas in 1836, first picked cotton for Grigsby and then grew it on several farms of his own near Beaumont. In addition to farming, many pioneers trapped the small animals on the riverbanks and in the woods, curing the hides and trading them for goods at the stores.

Two of the occupations of early Beaumonters during this postrevolutionary period had far-reaching implications for the future, eventually growing into industries that proved the abundance of the natural resources around them. The first to develop was the cattle-ranching industry. At first area farmers captured and raised the "mustang" cattle on the prairies simply for their families' subsistence, but soon they built their herds on the lush grasslands until their wealth was told in cattle. In 1839, 6,846 cattle were assessed as property on the Jefferson County tax rolls, and

by 1840 a few settlers were beginning to emerge as ranchers, periodically driving their herds east on the Opelousas Trail to the New Orleans market. Among these ranchers were Christian Hillebrandt, William Ashworth, David Garner (who also served a stint as Jefferson County's sheriff), McGuire Chaison, and James and William McFaddin. An offshoot of the ranching concern was Beaumont's first plant, Archie's Mill, in which carcasses of cattle were processed for tallow and hides and then thrown into the Neches, a practice which is said to have greatly increased the river's catfish population.

The second important industry to emerge in Beaumont during the postwar period was lumber. Cypress trees stood by the thousands in the Sabine and Neches river bottoms, providing an almost indestructible building material, and from their abundance grew an early shingle-manufacturing business. The cypress was cut in the woods, hauled by oxen to the river, and floated down to the town, where it was presawn into blocks, split with a froe and maul, then dressed with a drawknife. The finished shingles were shipped via schooner to Galveston and New Orleans.

Above
Farmer Luanza Calder owned 14 slaves and 400 head of cattle by 1860. Her husband Alexander settled in Beaumont in 1838, became clerk of the county court, and practiced law until his death in 1853. Courtesy, William T. Block.

Above
Christian Espar Hillebrandt came from Denmark, settling in the vicinity of Beaumont in the early 1830s. His 1835 land grant was 4,428 acres but within four years he owned more than 20,000 acres. Courtesy, Tyrrell Historical Library.

The vast East Texas stands of virgin pine and hardwood furnished another type of wood product. The logs were floated downriver or shipped by flatboat or keelboat to Beaumont, there to be made into boards, beams, or other building materials. (Because of the difficulty of moving these boats upriver again, most were dismantled in Beaumont and themselves sold as lumber.) The first "mill" in town was a whipsaw pit on the easternmost corner of land on the river at the foot of Main Street. It consisted simply of a large hole in the ground, over which a log could be propped. To saw the log, one man stood in the hole and handled one end of a crosscut saw, while another man perched atop the log and maneuvered the other end of the saw. This method of making lumber was eventually replaced by small horse-driven "muley" or "peck" mills, primitive operations in themselves but the unprepossessing beginnings of the thriving lumber industry of 19th-century Beaumont.

The forests provided more than just lumber for settlers. In 1845 a Connecticut Yankee by the name of John Jay French, a tanner by trade, brought his family to Beaumont and built his house, store, and tannery some miles north of town in a grove of the oak trees whose bark was so essential to the tanning process. He had already made at least two trips to Texas from his native New England, the first in 1832 when he traveled by 50-ton schooner down the Atlantic seaboard, after first placing on another ship most of the goods with which he planned to stock a store in Texas. Both vessels were caught in a storm; the ship carrying French was saved, but the one transporting his goods was sunk. His ship, mastless, limped into New Orleans for repairs, and from there French made his way via Galveston to Liberty, where he peddled his few remaining goods and returned to the East.

Above
John Jay and Sally French, born in Connecticut, chose to make their home in Beaumont. French built a successful tanning business and trading post and was one of the first settlers to grow rice in Jefferson County. Courtesy, Beaumont Heritage Society.

Undaunted, in the fall of 1835 he made his final trip to Texas, this time bringing his family by flatboat down the newly constructed Erie Canal and the Ohio and Mississippi rivers, thence overland to Opelousas. After being forced to remain in Opelousas for three years because of the Texas War for Independence, the Frenches finally resumed their journey to Texas by covered wagon along the Opelousas Trail. They first settled on French's original Mexican land grant on Flores Creek, now Taylor's Bayou, where French tried unsuccessfully to grow tobacco. Perhaps the location was unlucky; while camping on the bayou en route to his home one day, French was nearly dragged into the water by a large bull alligator, which had to be hit on the head with a provision box to be made to let him go. At any rate, determined to return to his New England profession of tanning, French in 1845 moved his family to the tract of land north of Beaumont. He was right in believing that his fortune was to be made there; within a few years he was supplying shoes, saddles, and other leather goods for most of Southeast Texas.

The settlers of Beaumont, as well as those in the rest of the Republic, were Texians, but before they had been Texians, they had been citizens of the United States. Most wanted Texas to be a part of the United States, and worked diligently toward that end. Beaumonters, like other settlers across the Republic, called a meeting in 1845 to draft a set of resolutions to annex Texas to the United States, appointing Frederick W. Ogden, an ardent annexationist, as chairman of the committee. In its resolutions, the group made a strong statement for annexation, expressing the belief that a failure to annex Texas to the United States would result in:

the final overthrow of the best and the brightest hopes of the human race, will extract the life blood from the tree of liberty, and cause her branches to wither, and finally crumble into anarchy and confusion.

Because Texas would enter as a slave state, many people in the United States were opposed to its joining the Union; however, after many false starts and delays, Texas became the 28th state on December 29, 1845. As he relinquished executive power to the new governor, James Pinckney Henderson, President Anson Jones spoke his valedictory to the citizens of the new state: "The final act in this great drama is now performed; the Republic of Texas is no more."

Above
The mantel of the restored John Jay French Trading Post holds the same clock that kept time for John Jay and Sally French. Photo by Wesley Norton. Courtesy, Beaumont Heritage Society.

Chapter III

Statehood, Civil War, and Reconstruction

*We are extremely pleased to witness many evidences
of the prosperity and improvement so apparent in our
immediate locality at the present time. The building
of saw mills, the construction of railroads, opening
farms, and the general influx of every rank; some of
wealth, all bidding fair to become useful citizens, and
of almost every avocation and calling, are the fore-
running events to the welfare and advancement of any
country wherein they exist.*
— *The* Beaumont Banner, *Beaumont's
first newspaper,
Tuesday, September 25, 1860*

Texas had no sooner entered the Union than it again found itself at war, a major cause being its own annexation. Mexico, refusing to acknowledge the right of any nation to claim territory it still considered to be its own, declared war upon the United States in 1846. Approximately 5,000 Texans (as the Texians had come to be known) answered the call to arms, this time as American citizens. Young men from Beaumont joined Company A of the Texas Rifles, or other military units, and trained to fight for their newly-acquired country. Since the war was of short duration, however, it affected relatively few Beaumonters; with the capture of Mexico City by General Winfield Scott in September of 1846, the tide of war turned in favor of the Americans. By the treaty of Guadalupe Hidalgo of 1848, Mexico acknowledged the Rio Grande as its northern boundary, thus tacitly accepting the annexation of Texas. After the war was over, the little town of Beaumont, unscathed by the previous conflict and as yet unshadowed by the conflagration to come, was allowed for a time to grow in peace.

Even though its population continued to increase, antebellum Beaumont remained a frontier town of log buildings and muddy, newly cleared streets, presenting an unprepossessing appearance to visitors. During the decade before the Civil War, a correspondent from the *Galveston Weekly News* named Henry Green stopped at Beaumont for a short time (or so he thought) on his way through East Texas. After first admitting to being "woefully disappointed in [his] expectations as to the appearance of the town and the condition of things generally," Green conceived a liking for the little frontier village, perhaps because of its inhabitants, who, he asserted, "for politeness and civility and attention to strangers, . . . are certainly remarkable." At any rate, Green remained in Beaumont for three and one-half years, becoming a schoolteacher, president of the Beaumont Debating Society, and, briefly, Jefferson County's district clerk. Under the pseudonym of "Hal," he periodically sent back to the *News* his succinct comments and observations of life in Beaumont in the decade preceding the Civil War.

During that time the center of the community developed, not at the original site of the Tevis homestead, but approximately half a mile downriver, where the sharp westward bend of the Neches at the foot of Main Street created a natural harbor. There a wooden wharf stood, where riverboats docked to load and unload their goods.

At this time very few of the streets laid out by Beaumont's founders had been cleared. Most of the area remained the dense thicket of pine, hardwood, and underbrush that Pulsifer had described upon his first sight of it. Main Street, an extension of the Jasper Road, came into town from the north, intersecting the east ends of Austin and Water streets before coming to a dead end at the river. Between Austin and Water, near the dock, was the old two-story Millard store, by then Cave Johnson's tavern and "hotel" (consisting of a few rooms upstairs over the tavern, where travelers could be put up for the night). A little way south of his establishment, on the riverbank, Johnson had planted a live oak switch, brought from Village Creek, that

Facing page
More than one boat was to proudly carry the name Neches Belle. *This drawing by local artist Natascha Bartnicki depicts a stern-wheeler of that name plying the Neches in the 1850s. Courtesy, Natascha Bartnicki.*

Above
The rifle was both the pioneer's tool in his search for food and his primary weapon in Texas wars. Beaumont gunsmith Robert J. Higgins, who was the father of Pattillo Higgins, made this rifle in the 1850s. Photo by Wesley Norton. Courtesy, Spindletop Museum.

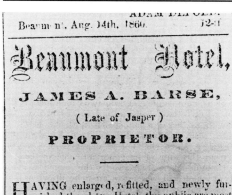

Beaumont, Aug. 14th, 1860.

Beaumont Hotel,

JAMES A. BARSE,

(Late of Jasper)

PROPRIETOR.

HAVING enlarged, refitted, and newly furnished the above Hotel, the public are most respectfully informed that it is now open for the accommodation of the traveling public.

The Proprietor contemplates additional improvements, during the coming season, and will spare no pains or expense to make it a first class House.

The table will always be supplied with the best the market affords and all the delicacies of the season.

By prompt attention to the wants of his guests, and a due regard for comfort, cleanliness, and good living, the proprietor hopes to deserve the confidence of the public.

J. A. BARSE.

Beaumont, Aug. 1st, 1860.

would later be known as the O'Brien Oak. East on Austin Street lay the Herring stores and the Red Front Saloon, operated by Hilmer Ruff, a German immigrant. This saloon, which was part log and part rough frame construction, had been slathered with bright red paint. According to a contemporary witness, "it stuck out like a sore thumb." On the east side of Main, at the foot of present-day Franklin Street, was located the blacksmith shop of Isaiah Junker.

A log schoolhouse stood in the woods at the present-day intersection of Pearl and College streets, and at the corner of Pearl and Milam, near the site where its modern-day counterpart now stands, was a low log building rented by the Jefferson County Board of Commissioners for use as a courthouse. Back of it, toward the river, was a cypress and gum swamp. (A new courthouse building was constructed on the same site sometime after 1854.)

A two-story log jail, its location uncertain because of its early disappearance, was the town's first public building, the prisoners occupying the upper story and the guards remaining on ground level. The security of the jail was questionable, however; according to one early account, "The jail building was not stout enough to shut within it anyone with a real desire to be elsewhere."

A little way to the northwest of town, in what came to be known as French Town, John Jay French had constructed next to his tannery a simple two-story Greek revival house, built of lumber and painted white, perhaps resembling the houses he had known from his childhood in Connecticut. It is thought to be the first house in the area to have a painted exterior.

Farther to the north, up the Neches River, lay an Indian camp, a reminder that just beyond the settled areas lay the wilderness. Indians, probably Alabamas, Coushattas, or Cherokees, who migrated to the area in the first quarter of the 19th century, appeared from time to time at Beaumont stores to trade the gold dust they carried in turkey quills for necessaries and for whiskey. (The origin of the gold, which the Indians evidently obtained somewhere in East Texas, is still a mystery.) Thomas F. Crawford, an early settler, remembered Indians during this era "carrying water in skins with their squaws trailing behind, their papooses strapped to their backs, down what is now Pearl Street."

Although settlers of Beaumont were still predominantly Anglo-Americans, beginning in the 1840s a new group of immigrants had joined them: the French Acadians,

Above

In 1860 the Beaumont Hotel advertised comfortable accommodations in the Beaumont Banner, *Beaumont's first newspaper. The hotel, above right, is shown in 1900. Courtesy, Chilton O'Brien.*

or Cajuns, as they came to be known, who would prove to have a significant economic and cultural influence on Southeast Texas. Evicted from Nova Scotia by the English in 1755, many of the Acadians settled in Louisiana, then began spilling across the Sabine into Texas, where farming and grazing land was more plentiful. To the names of Joseph and Michel Pivoto, Jonas B. Chaison, and Lefroy Guidry, who came before 1840, were added those of Emile and Sevan Broussard, Alexis Blanchette, John Jirou, and Joseph Hebert, who came to Jefferson County in 1842 and became one of the area's leading cattlemen. The numbers of Acadians swelled during the 1850s, and such French names as Trahan, Boudreaux, LaCour, Thibodeaux, Frugia, Leblanc, and Richard soon became part of the formerly predominantly Anglo roster of names in Jefferson County.

Anglo or Acadian, Danish or German, the early residents of the frontier settlement of Beaumont rarely had a moment's leisure. They labored from the early hours of the morning until dark, and after dark by candlelight, at the multitude of tasks required to maintain a frontier household. Of necessity, these households were largely self-sufficient; however, if a farmer occasionally needed an item that he could not grow or make himself, he walked or rode his horse or his mule to one of the riverside stores in Beaumont or to French's store in French Town.

Since Beaumont was near the coast, its citizens had somewhat readier access than did their Central or West Texas counterparts to items such as molasses, sugar, salt, tea, coffee, and tobacco, which were brought to Beaumont stores by boat, sometimes even by wagon, from Galveston and Sabine Pass. Because of the relative scarcity of cash, many transactions were made in vendibles; a ledger belonging to John Jay French during the 1850s shows that many Beaumonters, among them Alexander Calder, Nancy Tevis

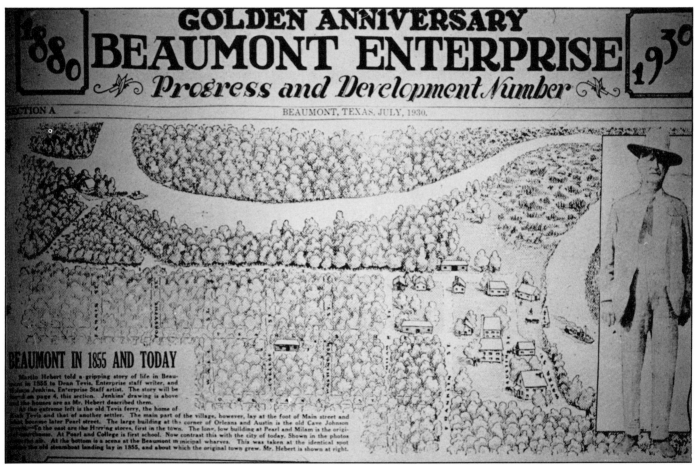

Above
Beaumont Enterprise *artist Holmes Jenkins made this drawing of Beaumont in 1855. The Noah Tevis house and ferry are at the upper left, the Cave Johnson tavern in the lower right, with the Herring stores above. The lone building in the center was the first school building in Beaumont. Courtesy, Lamar University Library.*

C. S. Pix, 1857

Lizie Thibedeaux, 1847

Noah Tevis, 1840

Wm. McFaddin, 1837

Joseph Roberts, 1839

Geo. C. O'Brian, 1891

S. C. Key, 1861

James T. White, 1820

Top left
Among the people of French descent to arrive in Beaumont before the Civil War was Jeff Chaison, descendant of Revolutionary War veteran Jonas Chaison and nephew of William McFaddin. After the war, in which he enlisted in Hood's Brigade, he became a successful rancher and realtor, and eventually served as county judge. Courtesy, Tyrrell Historical Library.

Bottom left
Among the young men who probably traded at French's Trading Post or Cave Johnson's store was E.C. Ogden, who later served as tax collector in Beaumont and sheriff of Jefferson County in the early 1870s. Courtesy, Tyrrell Historical Library.

Above
The cattle business was the mainstay of the Beaumont economy until lumbering emerged on a large scale. The Spanish introduced the practice of branding the cattle for identification. These brands spanned three quarters of a century, beginning with James T. White, the first cattleman in Jefferson County. Photo by Wesley Norton. Courtesy, Spindletop Museum.

Hutchinson, and William McFaddin, brought to his trading post raw deer and cow hides and barrels of corn and tallow to trade for such items as shoes, bridles, saddles, domestics, calico, buttons, combs, pins, razors, flour, and mosquito netting (a must for all Beaumont households). "Spirits" were also available at the store; French made his own whiskey, wine, and brandy, dipping the liquor from large storage barrels to sell by the pint, quart, or gallon.

Diversion for Beaumonters, when it came, was generally related to their work. In the early years of the settlement, a house or barn raising became a social gathering, with food and drink in abundance and sometimes even a fiddler to provide music for dancing. At one of these dances, two fiddlers played all night for $2.50 each, scraping out square dances, schottisches, waltzes, and quadrilles for the crowd's enjoyment. A manuscript in John Jay French's handwriting gives evidence that he performed magic tricks at frontier socials. Since he owned an accordion, it is reasonable to assume that he also sometimes played for the dancing.

In the years immediately preceding the Civil War, recreation in Beaumont acquired a little polish. A ballroom-dancing school was conducted in 1859 by James C. Clelland and in 1860 by William Harris, who styled himself as a "teacher of fashionable dances," charging $5 for women and $10 for men to participate in his course of dance lessons. Beaumonters responded enthusiastically, as Henry Green reported:

> *The citizens of this vicinity are attending our institution tri-weekly, having for its object the straightening of gauky underpinnings, defective spinal conformations, and the total eradication of time-honored reels, 'pigeon wings,' 'lock step,' and the whole catalogue of double-shuffle, go-along, thump-ta-bump movements of ancient times.*

Harris' students no doubt exhibited their newly acquired skills at such rare events as the occasional all-night ball given by a steamer captain aboard his ship in the Beaumont harbor, prior to his departure the next morning.

Holidays in Beaumont were occasions for celebration; Green vividly described a memorable Christmas spent with the family of McGuire Chaison. The first sign of the forthcoming festivities was a large dish of popcorn balls, accompanied, Green declared, with "no small share of that insepa-

rable concomitant of jubilation—great chit-chat and glorious gab. . . ." After the popcorn balls, he related, "Daddy McGuire killed the big rooster" and everyone partook of "all-hands-round eggnog. . . . Fiddling and dancing and a thousand other things took place—but this is enough for one Christmas." It was apparently enough for Green; he later declared that he was "sicker of eggnog than the whale was of Jonah."

Another excellent opportunity for social gatherings was county or district court, which convened once each quarter. Parties having an interest in the court proceedings stayed the weekend in the homes of friends or in Cave Johnson's inn, assembling for dancing Saturday night in the same courthouse in which the trial was being held.

The courts were always the scenes of much activity, for some of the ventures of early Beaumonters, social or otherwise, skirted the edges of the law, which during that Victorian time was both more narrow in itself than that of the present day and subject to more narrow interpretation. Several leading citizens were made to appear in court for "permitting card playing in the home" and were fined $10 for the offense. Fines for "adultery and fornication" were higher: $100 and one day in jail. One man considered to be a mulatto by his contemporaries preferred to pay his fine for fornication and continue to live with his white mate rather than marry and run the risk of being prosecuted for miscegenation.

The social and criminal event of the decade was the 1856 hanging of Jack Bunch, the 18-year-old mulatto who had been convicted of killing a deputy sheriff. (The murder was one incident in the series of wars that were occurring statewide during this time between the Regulators, a self-

Above
Residents of the Beaumont area found the ferries across the Neches River indispensable before the first bridge was built in 1924. Fees at Parsons Collier's Ferry in 1862 were 25 cents a wheel for carts and carriages, 25 cents for man and horse, $6 for team, wagon, and all persons aboard, and 2 cents per head of cattle. Courtesy, Sam Houston Regional Library.

appointed vigilante group among whom Bunch was numbered, and the Moderators, a band of men who organized to oppose the Regulators.) A huge crowd of people gathered at the courthouse square for the execution as though it were a festive occasion. Sheriff Jack Ingalls conducted the execution, requesting Bunch to mount the ladder to the makeshift gallows, then, when he complied, kicking it from under the unfortunate man.

Beaumonters, like members of any frontier community, were eager to establish religious centers as soon as possible. During the 1850s Beaumont was a part of the Alligator Circuit, so called because ministers who traveled to and from the little settlements in Southeast Texas and Southwest Louisiana killed the numerous alligators they found on the swampy trails, selling the hides to supplement their meager incomes. Even though no church building existed in Beaumont until later years, the populace met regularly in the courthouse on Sundays, hearing the preaching of lay ministers if an ordained man were not present. Labels were not important in the early days; a minister of any faith tended an interdenominational flock. The Reverend John Fletcher Pipkin, who arrived with his family in the early 1850s, preached in homes, brush arbors, and borrowed public buildings, ministering to all denominations alike.

As evidenced by the lone log schoolhouse so proudly shown to Pulsifer by Joseph Grigsby in 1835, Beaumonters also had a care for the education of their youngsters; by the early 1850s they supported several private schools. Within the area of the town itself, institutions such as the school at Pearl and College, taught for a time by Jefferson County's sometime sheriff James Ingalls, and the school on Jasper Road, taught by Henry Green, served more than one family. Settlers such as the McFaddins and the Broussards, who lived on outlying homesteads, hired "live-in" teachers for

Above
This frame building was started in 1854 and accepted by county officials as the courthouse three years later. Photographed in 1860, left to right, are Captain Peter D. Stockholm (?), next two unknown, B.J. Johnson, Savinee Blanchette, George Millard (?), unknown, Ira Bordages, Jim Ingalls, Charles McFaddin, Sab Landrum, Tom Langham, and the Reverend John F. Pipkin. Courtesy, Business Men's Studio.

their offspring and any other children who lived nearby.

In February 1854, the Jefferson County Board of Commissioners established five school districts in Jefferson County, appointing trustees for each district; McGuire Chaison and Dr. G.W. Hawley were trustees for District Number One at Beaumont. In 1858 A.N. Vaughn founded the Beaumont Male and Female Academy, which offered primary geography, higher mathematics, and painting in addition to its basic curriculum of reading, spelling, writing, and arithmetic.

In addition to contributing to their town's internal development, Beaumonters were improving communication with the outside world. The Galveston and Sabine Bay Stage, owned and operated by George Bryan, originally of Beaumont but by 1846 a resident of Galveston, made a round trip every week through Bolivar, Sabine Pass, Galveston, and Beaumont, charging six dollars for a one-way fare. By the 1850s postal routes had been established, linking Beaumont with Woodville, Jasper, Galveston, Sabine Pass, and other area settlements; mail also came by way of packets from Sabine Pass, Galveston, and New Orleans.

River traffic during the 1850s steadily increased in volume. During that time the Morgan Steamship Lines began making regular once-a-week stops at Sabine Pass. In 1848 the first steamer had sailed up the Neches to Bevilport, a small settlement at the junction of the Neches and the

Angelina, and after that date steamboats had continued to grow in number and importance. Stern-wheelers such as the *Neches Belle,* the *Uncle Ben,* the *Rough and Ready,* the *Mary Falvey,* the *Doctor Massie,* the *Pearl Plant* and particularly the *Sunflower* dominated the Neches, bringing cotton and hides downriver and other items of trade upriver. The largest steamboats based at Beaumont were the *Josiah H. Bell* and the enormous 200-foot *Florilda.* These two boats did not engage in ordinary river commerce, but in transporting ties, rails, and other materials to the construction sites of the new railroads, ironically, in doing so, helping to write their own death warrants.

The railroads, destined eventually to supplant the riverboats as a method of transportation, made their appearance in Southeast Texas in the latter 1850s. The

Above
John F. Pipkin, lay Methodist minister, was pastor to people of all faiths for many years, being the only resident preacher in the area. During the Civil War Pipkin tended the physical and spiritual needs of the wounded who were treated in the courthouse. After the war he and his son-in-law, Dr. M.G. Haltom, bought and operated a sawmill. This versatile man also served as county judge during the last decade of his life. Courtesy, First United Methodist Church.

Above
Methodists and Baptists, who had intermittently shared space and worship services for many years, built this church jointly soon after the Civil War. Baptist layman John M. Long led the singing, and lay Methodist minister John F. Pipkin preached. Men and women were admitted through separate entrances and sat on opposite sides of the sanctuary. Courtesy, First United Methodist Church.

BEAUMONT MALE AND FEMALE ACADEMY.

The second session of this Academy will commence July 23rd, 1860.

Rates of Tuition Per Session of Five Months.

Orthography, Reading, Writing, Primary Geography, Mental Arithmetic............$10 00
Geography, Higher Arithmetic, English Grammar, History, Composition...........$15 00
Higher Sciences and Mathematics, French and Latin.................................$20 00
Drawing and Painting, each...............$12 00
Music..$25,00

Tuition charged from date of entrance.

No deduction, except in cases of protracted sickness. Board can be had in private families at from $8 to $10 per month.

The building is commodious, and situated in a secluded portion of the Town. It is to be hoped that parents desiring for their children the advantages of a sound moral discipline and a thorough Education, will sustain this school, it being the object of the undersigned to make it in every respect worthy of their patronage.

F. O. YATES, PRINCIPAL.

Beaumont, May 29th, 1860.

SABINE PASS ADVERTISEMENTS.

Eastern Texas Railroad in 1857 began construction of a route from Sabine Pass to Beaumont, but halted a few miles south of town when the supply of materials was exhausted. The next year work was begun in Houston on the Texas and New Orleans Railroad, which by 1861 had completed track from Houston to Beaumont and was laying track to the new settlement of Orange on the Sabine River.

It soon became apparent that the growth of Beaumont's young lumber industry would heavily depend upon these railroads; the cost of transporting lumber by water from Beaumont to other points was so exorbitant that it was actually cheaper for builders to import it from the East

Coast. The lower shipping costs offered by the railroads would enable local lumbermen to offer competitive prices. As it was, the sale of lumber from the mills in Beaumont was largely restricted to local markets, because only a small percentage of production could be profitably exported.

Even without adequate methods of exportation, the lumber industry in Beaumont made significant progress during the antebellum period. In 1856 William Phillips and Loving G. Clark built a steam mill at a site on Brakes Bayou, originally intended by the town's founders for that specific purpose. Soon after, in 1857, John R. Ross and James R. Alexander transported overland a mill from the Trinity River, setting it up in the neigh-

Above
This 1860 advertisement for the Beaumont Male and Female Academy shows the rates and coursework for the Academy's second year. County commissioners disbursed funds for the education of indigent children at the rate of 10 cents a day per child. Courtesy, Chilton O'Brien.

Above
Pioneer lumberman John W. Keith had enlisted in the Confederate army by the age of 16. After the war he became a partner in Long and Company. Courtesy, Tyrrell Historical Library.

borhood of the first mill on Brakes Bayou near present-day Pine Street (at that time part of the Jasper Road). This mill housed a "selfsetter," an innovation that was the wonder of all who saw it. In the *Galveston Weekly News*, Green marveled at the gadget that was revolutionizing the lumber business:

> *I was shown yesterday a novel invention, a selfsetter at Ross and Alexander's mill, with which the logs are set to the saw, and which reduced the boards to an exact precision in width and thickness at both ends, so that there's no use in house carpenters swearing about clumsily-sawed stuff, if they get a supply of this company's manufacture. . . . All that you have to do is to roll the log upon the carriage, drive in your mainstays or grappling irons, . . . put on steam, and then go to dinner, and by the time you get back the log is slabbed, sawn up, shoved out of the mill, stacked up, and the price marked on the topmost plank—and all done by steam! After this, who will say that steam is not a wheelhorse?*

Unfortunately, the mill burned, along with 60,000 feet of lumber, in early 1859. The owners then sold the site and the salvaged machinery to Captain James M. Long, a Georgian who had settled that year in Beaumont, and his brother-in-law from Louisiana, Francis Lafayette Carroll. Another sawmill, bought in 1859 by Otto Ruff from the Steadman Foundry in Indiana, was shipped by boat via New Orleans to Beaumont. This mill was sold several times, eventually evolving into the Reliance Lumber Company, which, with Long's company and its offshoots, the Beaumont Lumber Company and the Texas Tram and Lumber Company, would comprise Beaumont's four lumber giants during the last quarter of the 19th century.

The emergence of another industry in Beaumont was unknowingly predicted by the *Texas Almanac* of 1858 when it said of the area surrounding the city: "Much of the soil is swampy, and well suited to the culture of rice." Brought from Louisiana about 1849 by Acadians such as Joe Hebert, who was one of its earliest growers, rice, like corn, was at first grown in rows, only for family consumption. Farmers never irrigated their rice but depended entirely upon the rain to provide sufficient moisture to sprout the seeds; hence, the crop came to be known as "providence rice." Gradually, as farmers became aware that the rich black clay around Beaumont was much better suited to the cultivation of rice than of cotton, the crop began to assume ever-

Above
Francis Lafayette Carroll, father of George W. Carroll, entered the lumber business with James M. Long before the Civil War. After the war, in partnership with his brother-in-law William A. Fletcher and Joseph A. Carroll, he organized the Texas Tram and Lumber Company. Courtesy, W.T. Block.

Above, middle and right
James M. Long, who settled in Beaumont on the eve of the Civil War, joined F.L. Carroll in the purchase of the Ross and Alexander Lumber Company. The war, in which Long enlisted, interfered with their plans, and after the war they established separate companies. Long died prematurely but his widow Theresa helped carry on the business. Courtesy, First Baptist Church and Mrs. Ed E. Carroll.

increasing importance to Southeast Texas.

In 1860 Beaumont took a vital step in its evolution from frontier town to city. Schoolteacher A.N. Vaughn forsook his teaching profession that year to become editor and publisher of Beaumont's first newspaper, the *Beaumont Banner*, also for a time filling the post of mayor of the town. Called by a fellow area newspaper "an uncommonly neat, spicy, and ably conducted sheet," the *Banner* during its brief existence enjoyed a circulation of 400. It served as a community conscience: "That a house adapted to the worship of God is needed in Beaumont, none will deny. . . . Let us then build such an edifice, and thereby show our deep sense of the value and importance of cultivating and fostering the tender sensibilities of human nature." It proudly announced progress: "Our schoolhouse, which has been so long talked of, is now in reality being built, and will without a doubt, be completed by the first of April. This house, which has been so badly needed, will be, when completed, . . . an ornament to our town." And finally, the *Banner* also reflected the personalities of Beaumonters. The August 14, 1860, edition carried an admonishment from tavern and grocery store owner Cave Johnson, apparently a colorful character: "Notice is hereby given to all persons owing bar bills at Cave Johnson's Grocery, to pay up on or before the 26th of this month. Come to time, gentlemen, and pay for your tea."

Even while they enjoyed their community's progress, Beaumonters, like other Americans, realized that their time of peace would soon be over. On the national scene, the tension between North and South, primarily over the question of slavery, had been steadily escalating into open conflict. Texans were about to exchange their newly-acquired statehood in the Union for that of another: the Confederacy. For the third time in 26 years, Beaumonters would be called upon to furnish men and supplies for a war effort.

In 1859 Governor Sam Houston, a pro-Union conservative opposed to secession, won the governor's race in what was to be his last political battle, but his opposition, the radical pro-Southern faction, soon gained statewide support. Abraham Lincoln was elected President of the United States in 1860; in Texas, where his name did not even appear on the ticket, a strident majority of 47,548 Texas voters defiantly cast their ballots for John C. Breckinridge, the states-rights candidate. On December 20 of that year, South Carolina seceded from the Union; Texas followed suit in the spring of 1861. Houston, furious at the actions of the Texas secession convention, refused to take the oath of allegiance to the Confederacy, whereupon the convention declared the

Above
Woodson Pipkin, one of 13 slaves owned by the Reverend John F. Pipkin, served Reverend Pipkin as valet and bodyguard during the Civil War. Woodson Pipkin was founder with Charles Charlton of the first black school in Beaumont and was one of the founders and eventually pastor of the African Methodist Episcopal Church. Courtesy, Fayetta Donovan.

Above
Beaumont's first weekly newspaper, the Beaumont Banner, *had to depend on surrounding communities for advertising support. A chilling article, typical of Southern newspapers, analyzes the unique behavior of Negro slaves, attempting to help owners improve the efficiency of slave labor. Courtesy, Chilton O'Brien.*

office of governor vacant, elevating Lieutenant Governor Edward Clark to the position.

The population of Beaumont, like that in the rest of the state, was composed for the most part of immigrants from the Old South. Consequently, sympathies of Beaumonters lay irrevocably with the Southern cause. They heatedly discussed the national situation at public gathering places and crowded the dock, anxiously awaiting news, when the mail packets came in from Sabine Pass or Galveston. The *Banner* carried impassioned editorials supporting the secessionist cause and castigating Governor Houston for his pro-Union stand: "To what awakening hast thou led our once passive intellect; and to what base, selfish, and unworthy subterfuges is thy name, fame and talents prostituted?" In the secession election in early 1861, 141 Beaumonters voted with the rest of Texas to secede from the Union; only 12 wished to remain a part of it.

When on April 12, 1861, Confederate forces fired upon Fort Sumter, the Civil War became a reality. Beaumonters began preparing for war. City government not only ground to an abrupt halt, but the *Banner* ceased publication as Mayor Vaughn left to enlist in Company F, Fifth Texas

Regiment, later known as Hood's Brigade. His example was emulated by many others, including Jefferson Chaison, the Wiess brothers, Mark, William, Massena, and Valentine, and William A. Fletcher, a young Beaumonter who was shingling a roof when he learned of the fall of Fort Sumter. Fletcher hurriedly completed the roof in order to join Hood's Brigade; however, a serious injury at the Second Battle of Manassas later necessitated his transfer to a cavalry unit, where he remained for the duration of the war.

George W. O'Brien, a young Beaumont lawyer, also enlisted in Company F as Fletcher's unit left Beaumont for Virginia. O'Brien, the son of storekeeper and stage-line owner George Bryan, had come to Beaumont in 1852, changing his name from "Bryan," as his father spelled it, back to its original Irish form of "O'Brien" and becoming licensed to practice law in Jefferson County a bare three months before he joined the Confederate army. He had strenuously opposed secession, but nevertheless felt it his duty to support the decision of the majority.

When O'Brien reached Virginia, he contracted a severe case of measles and received a medical discharge. After his return to Beaumont, however, he recovered sufficiently to

Above, left to right
William, Mark, and Valentine Wiess enlisted in Hood's Brigade promptly upon the secession of Texas in 1861. After the war Captain William Wiess was involved in steamboating, Mark was a successful speculator, and Valentine bought out William in 1873. Each brother was prominent in Beaumont business life into the 20th century. Courtesy, Tyrrell Historical Library.

reenlist in the army. He was given the commission of captain and the command of Company E of Likens' Battalion, Texas Volunteers, for which he recruited in Beaumont and neighboring settlements.

In 1861 Federal ships began to blockade the Texas coast, and in 1862 Galveston was captured by Union gunboats, bringing the war much closer to Beaumonters. Because of the Union's desire not only to destroy Texas as a Confederate supply center but also to split the Trans-Mississippi South, the Gulf Coast of Texas was particularly vulnerable to enemy attack. Beaumont, the largest community on the Neches, just above strategically-located Sabine Pass, was potentially important to the Federals. Aware of this grim fact, Beaumonters and their Southeast Texas neighbors roused to a spirited defense of the coast, which one historian has called "one of the most brilliant chapters in the story of the Confederacy." Confederate blockade runners, speedy, shallow-draft steamers and schooners painted light gray, ran the gauntlet of the Federal blockade ships, transporting contraband goods to and from Beaumont and the surrounding area. Many riverboat captains were hired by the Confederacy to command the blockade runners, realizing a fantastic profit for their daring. Sailing at night, utilizing their intimate knowledge of the treacherous Sabine Lake and the outlying coastlines of Texas and Louisiana, these masters easily eluded the clumsy Union sailing vessels waiting off-shore to stop them.

An epidemic of yellow fever, brought to Sabine Pass by the blockade-running British steamer *Victoria* in July 1862, raged from August to October of that year. Fifty people died there, and most of the rest were evacuated. Dr. G.W. Hawley, who had come from Beaumont to tend to the stricken inhabitants of the little town, also succumbed to the illness.

While Sabine Pass was thus unable to defend itself, on September 24, 1862, three Union gunboats appeared off the coast, firing intermittently at the town. They made no attempt to take it; their fear of yellow fever proved to be an effective deterrent. As a result of the panic induced by the presence of the ships, however, several convalescents from Sabine Pass broke quarantine and took refuge in Beaumont. The commanding officer of the Houston Sub-Military District, Colonel X.B. DeBray, ordered the southern end of the town to be placed under quarantine, but, he wrote, "I doubt . . . the efficiency of the measure and apprehend that the disease will spread all over town." DeBray's fears were

Top
William A. Fletcher moved to Beaumont in 1856 and was engaged in carpentry when the Civil War began. After the war he joined the Carrolls in the Texas Tram and Lumber Company. It was his genius as a skilled mechanic and millwright that contributed greatly to the success of the companies with which he was associated. Courtesy, Tyrrell Historical Library.

Bottom
As a boy in 1850, George W. O'Brien, working for his father, brought the mail by stage from Beaumont to Galveston. He later became a lawyer, but interrupted his practice to join Spaight's Battalion in defending the Texas coast. His many interests included publication of the Neches Valley News, *the* Beaumont News-Beacon, *service as county clerk and town alderman, and partnership in the Gladys City Oil Company. Courtesy, Tyrrell Historical Library.*

realized; "yellow jack" broke out in Beaumont, killing at least eight people.

Troops from Jefferson, Chambers, Liberty, and other counties trained in Beaumont, among them Captain O'Brien's company, formerly of Likens' Battalion, now of Spaight's Texas Regiment. They camped on the hill south of town, near the sour springs, which had by then acquired the name of Spindletop because of a nearby cypress tree, shaped like the spindle on a spinning wheel, which for years had served as a landmark to boatmen. Reportedly, while Captain O'Brien was camped at Spindletop Springs, he happened to notice that globules of natural petroleum collected on the surface of their waters, and that when he listened closely, he could hear the hiss of gas escaping from the earth. Perhaps even then Captain O'Brien had a premonition of its importance, but the rumble of Spindletop was still to make itself heard.

Camp Spindletop, a collection of hastily erected tents and lean-tos, was used not only as a training ground but, during the yellow fever epidemic of 1862, as a hospital. Several soldiers died and were reputedly buried in unmarked graves on the hill.

On New Year's Day, 1863, Confederate forces under General J. Bankhead Magruder regained possession of Galveston, but the rest of the year portended ill for the Confederacy. Southern defeats at Gettysburg and Vicksburg marked the turning point of the war, releasing Federal troops for service elsewhere, including an invasion of Texas. It would soon become apparent to the Southern command that there would be a coastal offensive, not at Galveston, which by this time was well fortified, but at Sabine Pass.

Union strategy included using gunboats to incapacitate Fort Griffin, Sabine Pass' small, undermanned mud fortress; landing troops; proceeding overland to seize a

Above
Several companies of Colonel A.W. Spaight's Battalion, later known as Hood's Brigade, camped at Spindletop Springs in 1862 while guarding the approaches to Texas. One of the soldiers sketched his version of the camp where, incidentally, some noticed the peculiar gases and liquids working their way to the surface of the springs. Courtesy, Sam Houston Regional Library.

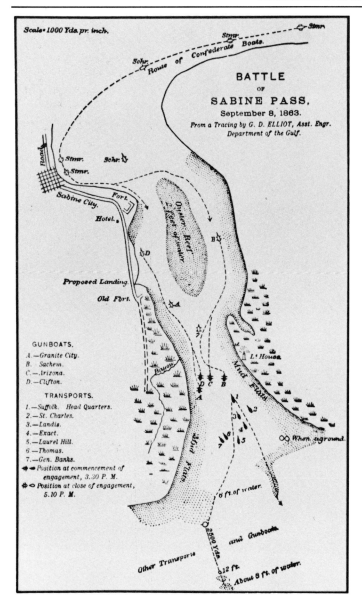

to serve in the vanguard of the attack. With Lieutenant Frederick Crocker in command, the expedition was launched in early September, 1863.

Meanwhile, frantic preparations were taking place on the Texas coast. General Magruder, learning of the impending invasion, gave orders to fortify Sabine Pass. A supply depot was established at Beaumont and the steamers *Josiah H. Bell* and *Uncle Ben* were refitted as "cotton-clad" gunboats; that is, their vital parts were protected by cotton bales stacked on the decks. Troops began concentrating at Fort Griffin, where Lieutenant Richard W. Dowling, an Irish barkeeper from Houston, was in command.

On the morning of September 8, Federal gunboats appeared off the Pass and opened fire on the fort. Dowling and his 47 men, who had practiced for long hours at their artillery marksmanship, returned no answer to the gunfire as long as the Union vessels were outside their range. About three o'clock that afternoon, however, the gunboats began advancing, showering upon Fort Griffin, according to a contemporary observer, "a most galling and terrific fire. . . ."

When the ships passed the channel stakes marking the range of their guns, Dowling's men opened fire with deadly accuracy. The gunfire quickly crippled the *Sachem*, grounding her on a mud flat. A well-aimed shell blew up her boilers, scalding many crewmen and forcing others overboard. With the *Sachem* out of commission, the artillerymen of Fort Griffin turned their guns on the *Clifton*. As Lieutenant Crocker, aboard the *Clifton*, attempted to posi-

point, probably Beaumont, on the Texas and New Orleans railroad line; then pressing on to Houston and its important railroad system.

The Federal orders for the attack were issued August 31, 1863, for a force of 4,000 men to "effect a landing at Sabine Pass, Texas, for military occupation. . . ." The Union command, having learned well to beware of the shallows of Sabine Lake, named four light-draft gunboats, the *Clifton*, the *Arizona*, the *Granite City*, and the *Sachem*

Above
This drawing shows the position of the Union gunboats which met such devastating defeat at Sabine Pass in 1863. The Sachem *and the* Clifton *ran aground and were eventually captured. The* Arizona *and the* Granite City *escaped in spite of being temporarily grounded, whereupon all Union forces withdrew. Courtesy, Timothy Spell.*

Above
The Union ship Clifton *sank as a result of the cannonade from Lieutenant Dowling's men inside Fort Griffin. In 1912 Beaumonters wrenched the handwrought walking beam from the* Clifton's *wreckage and eventually installed it in Pipkin Park overlooking the Port of Beaumont. Photo by Wesley Norton.*

tion his vessel to fire broadside at the fort, she also ran aground. A shell struck her tiller rope, then exploded her steam drum, whereupon Crocker surrendered. The cotton-clad *Uncle Ben*, lying in the Pass near the fort, steamed over to the *Clifton*, its men helping Dowling take prisoners and transport them to Beaumont. The *Arizona*, the *Granite City*, and the rest of the Union forces, stymied by such dogged opposition, retreated to New Orleans. The Confederate victory at the Battle of Sabine Pass had prevented the invasion of the Texas coast.

The last battles fought by men of the Beaumont area were in Louisiana. Andrew McFaddin, a Beaumonter, was killed at the Battle of Bayou Fordoche. At the Battle of Calcasieu Pass, fought on May 6, 1864, Confederate forces, including Captain George W. O'Brien's Company, captured two Union gunboats, one of which, the *Granite City*, had previously escaped capture at Sabine Pass. Taking part in this battle were several other Beaumonters, including hotel owner Cave Johnson.

The victory at Calcasieu Pass boosted Southern morale, but not for long. The battle was won, but the war, for the South, was lost. In May 1865, a month after General Lee's surrender at Appomattox, General Edmund Kirby Smith, commander of the Confederate Trans-Mississippi Department, boarded a federal ship in Galveston Harbor to surrender his command. Galveston and its neighbor, Sabine Pass, were the final bastions of Southern defiance, being the last to lower the Confederate flag.

Once again Beaumonters returned home from war, this time to face formidable impediments to the resumption of their everyday lives. The first Reconstruction Act, passed by a vengeful Republican Congress, established military rule in Texas and disfranchised those who had been loyal Confederates. By the summer of 1865, Union troops occupied Beaumont. Yankee soldiers ran the government, and freed blacks had charge of ballot boxes. George

Above
Nathan Gilbert, who came to Jefferson County about the time of the Civil War, served as the Confederate cotton agent at Sabine Pass. He was the ancestor of John N. Gilbert, who had interests in ranching, rice, lumber, and eventually oil. Courtesy, Ruth and Florence Chambers.

Above
Lieutenant Richard "Dick" Dowling, born in Ireland, was a hero after his astonishing victory over superior Union forces at Sabine Pass. The monument in Fort Griffin State Park memorializes him and his men, many of them from Beaumont. Courtesy, Business Men's Studio.

O'Brien, home from his honorable service in Louisiana, feared "the current of malice and oppression . . . about to engulf us."

Reconstruction was made even more difficult in Beaumont, as in the rest of the South, by the fact that the economy had slowed almost to a standstill. Cotton exports had dropped; the railroads, neglected since the beginning of the war, lay in a state of disuse and disrepair. The sawmills had stood inactive for the latter part of the war, and even the

number of cattle in Jefferson County had been depleted because of the Confederate army's need for beef.

The South, and Beaumont, were invaded by carpetbaggers and their ilk, determined to batten upon Southern misfortune. One particular carpetbagger, a clock-tinkerer known only as "Charley Yank," made the mistake of trying to bribe Uncle Straud, the elderly black servant of John Jay French, to admit him secretly into the trading post to steal French's gold. The Yankee did not realize the extent of Uncle Straud's loyalty to French; when in the dead of night the old servant unlocked the door for Charley Yank, he led him into ambush. French's sons and several of their neighbors, hiding in the second-floor store area, fired their guns in unison, shooting Charley Yank where he stood, burying him, according to family legend, "while he was a-battin' his eyes."

Beaumonters, managing as best they could during the bleak postwar years, gradually began to build up their herds of cattle and to work their farms again, adjusting to the new lack of slave labor by hiring field hands or by doing the work themselves. When he returned to Beaumont, W.A. Fletcher "gathered up father's old carpenter tools and went on a job at a dollar and a half per day, about one hundred feet from the place where [he] left off work." George O'Brien, unable to make a living as an attorney in postwar Beaumont, turned for a time to the manufacture of cypress shingles before he was able to return to the practice of law.

In 1867, 200 armed men, led by Captain Edward I. Kellie of Jasper, declared themselves to be delegates to the Democratic convention being held in Beaumont, announcing their determination to "restore their citizenship and their right to vote and to place the names of white Democrats and Southern patriots on the ballot." They succeeded in wresting the ballot box from the company of northern militia and freed blacks (one of whom was the election judge), thereby precipitously ending carpetbag rule in Beaumont.

In that same year General Philip H. Sheridan, the harsh warden of the Fifth Military District, which included Texas, was replaced by General W.S. Hancock, a man far more lenient toward the South than Sheridan had been. Hancock allowed civil officials to resume their interrupted jobs, and disfranchised voters to register once again. On April 16, 1870, the military commander of Texas, General J.J. Reynolds, restored power to the civil government. For Texas, Reconstruction was over.

Above
Levi Simpson Hatch fought against the Confederacy at the Battle of Sabine Pass. Many years later he returned to Beaumont by way of Louisiana and worked as a janitor at First Baptist Church. Courtesy, Tyrrell Historical Library.

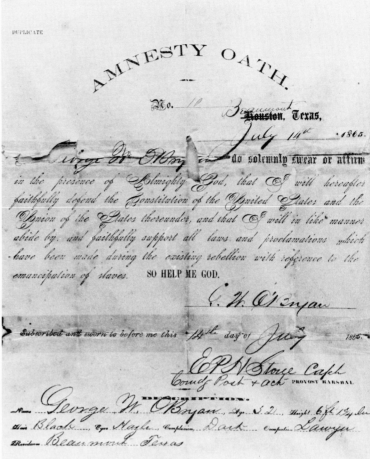

Two prophetic incidents occurred during the Reconstruction period that augured well for Beaumont's economic future. One was an item appearing in *Flake's Daily Galveston Bulletin*, July 11, 1866.

Three reliable gentlemen visited our city this week, informing us of some facts concerning what they suppose to be the existence of petroleum in the section of country lying between the Angelina and Neches rivers. [They] say that there is a wide belt of country running east and west through Texas that will one day yield an immense amount of oil.

The other was a letter received by George O'Brien from a friend in Liberty, A.P. Tarwell, instructing O'Brien to buy all the land in Jefferson County with "Sour Lake water or

Sour Lake tar'' on it. He continued:

If you manage this thing judiciously ... there is a larger sum of gold dollars in it for us than we have seen or heard of in our whole lives. ... The great excitement of the age is oil *.... What is the use toiling and struggling with aching brains and weary hands for bread, when* gold *so temptingly invites you to reach out and clutch it?*

O'Brien declined his friend's generous offer of a partnership in the fabulous venture, but perhaps the idea suggested by Tarwell, as well as his own previous experiences at Camp Spindletop, served as impetus for his involvement in the search for oil on the hill south of Beaumont a quarter of a century later.

Above
Mrs. Nora Lee Haltom, daughter of John F. Pipkin, was born in Arkansas and moved to Jefferson County with her family about 1850. She served as postmistress in Beaumont during the Civil War. Courtesy, W.T. Block.

Above
George W. O'Brien had vigorously opposed secession, but later committed himself fully to the Confederate cause. On July 14, 1865, he signed this amnesty oath. Courtesy, Chilton O'Brien.

Chapter IV

Lumber and Locomotives

In less that two months, our mills will be shipping 30 car loads of lumber per day. The lumber, shingles and ties shipped from this point now average $43,000 per month or $516,000 per annum. That beats cotton all hollow. . . .

— Beaumont Lumberman, *reprinted*
Galveston Weekly News, *January 18, 1878*

In spite of A.P. Tarwell's prediction, it was not yet oil but lumber that, with the help of the young railroads, was to banish the last bitter dregs of Reconstruction, giving to Beaumont a golden era of prosperity in the last quarter of the 19th century. With the badly needed rail transportation providing not only a means of exporting the milled long-leaf yellow pine but also a full access to its source, the still boundless East Texas forests, the Beaumont lumber industry flourished. It reached its zenith just before the turn of the century in the enormous production of its great sawmills. The wealth from this lumber boom created in town a lumber barony, which infused the town with new energy and inaugurated a style of living commensurate with its status. With the help of this group, Beaumont was transformed from a frontier settlement into a gracious little city, with a few elegant Victorian homes, a developing municipal consciousness, and a budding cultural scene.

The railroads did not recover immediately from the effects of the Civil War. Much of the Eastern Texas Railroad had been destroyed, its rails and ties ripped up in 1863 to be used in the construction of Fort Griffin. The Texas and New Orleans (locally known as the T&NO), although still in existence, was in an advanced state of disrepair. In 1876, however, the year that the last of the federal troops were withdrawn from Beaumont, Orange, and Sabine Pass, a new state constitution restored the right of Texas to issue land grants to railroads, and they began to rebuild.

The lumbermen, realizing how completely the hope of expanding their industry lay in obtaining adequate rail transportation, actively abetted the recovery process. On November 13, 1876, James Long and his father, Davis Long, partners in the Long and Company sawmill, sold for one dollar to the newly reorganized T&NO line a 150-foot right-of-way between Pearl and Orleans streets in Beaumont to be used for building a terminal. The T&NO was reopened that same year, with a depot located at the corner of Pearl and Crockett streets; thereafter, Beaumont's business district began to cluster around it, moving away from the old site downriver. It provided a vital trade link from Beaumont to the older Eastern states as well as to the growing young city of Houston, which soon after the war was recognized as the railroad center of Texas.

From 1880 to 1883, Herman and Augustus Kountze, two New York bankers who had acquired many thousands of acres of East Texas timberland, rebuilt the old Eastern Texas Railroad from Sabine Pass to Beaumont, eventually extending it north through the pine woods. The first regular run of the Sabine and East Texas was made on February 2, 1881; thereafter, trains ran daily from Sabine Pass to Beaumont, then up through innumerable small Texas sawmill towns, such as Kountze, Warren, and Hillister, to the end of the line at Rockland.

Facing page
Around the turn of the century, this steam log skidder operated in a Beaumont pine forest. The skidder was invented by millwright William A. Fletcher. Courtesy, Business Men's Studio.

Above
This Baldwin locomotive is one of those that expedited the movement of logs from forest to mills, thus spurring the huge growth of Beaumont sawmills. The wood-burning engine, designed in 1866 by M.N. Forney, was very practical on the rails that extended to every corner of the woods. Courtesy, Business Men's Studio.

Above
The "Old Mother Hubbard," as this Southern Pacific locomotive was fondly called, pulled freight and passengers to Sabine Pass in the 1890s. When Spindletop brought in boomers, this engine carried some of the human overflow to the famous Windsor Hotel at Sabine Pass. Courtesy, Tyrrell Historical Library.

After absorbing the Sabine and East Texas Railroad in 1882, the T&NO eventually became part of the great Southern Pacific intercontinental railway system. By 1890 the Southern Pacific Company had built in Beaumont a new brick roundhouse with 14 stalls and, according to a contemporary newspaper account, "one of the handsomest depot buildings in the state." This depot was designed especially for the Beaumont climate; its enormous overhanging eaves kept the building and its occupants dry on rainy days, even when the doors and windows were left open.

In 1896 entrepreneur and budding lumberman John Henry Kirby built a small railroad called the Gulf, Beaumont and Kansas City line, reaching from Beaumont to Kirbyville in East Texas. It was later extended as far as Longview, Texas, and DeRidder, Louisiana, and was absorbed by the Santa Fe system. In an attempt to find a short route to ship Kansas wheat to the coast, a Kansas City promoter named Arthur Stillwell built a railway in 1897 called the Kansas City Southern, running through Beaumont to the Gulf. Stillwell laid out a 4,000-acre townsite on the shores of Sabine Lake to serve as its terminus, and the town, Port Arthur, was named for him.

The proliferation of the railroads removed the only obstacle to the growth of the lumber industry, and its proponents quickly seized the opportunity. During the 1870s and 1880s lumber production increased astonishingly, and several new mills were established in Beaumont.

Long and Company, located between Brake's Bayou and Pine Street (the Jasper Road), by now an established lumber mill, had become a family concern under the leadership of James Long and his father, Davis Long. The partnership included Davis Long's sons-in-law, W.A. Fletcher, John W. Keith, brothers Joseph A. Carroll and Frank L. Carroll (with whom Long had originally bought the mill), and Frank Carroll's son-in-law, Jehu Frank Keith, who with his brother John L. Keith was also John W. Keith's nephew. From this intricately interwoven family alliance came a dynasty of lumber barons, a powerful new group whose presence was strongly felt in Beaumont.

J. Frank Keith, who married Frank Carroll's daughter Alice in 1882, was to have a particularly brilliant financial career, as would George W. Carroll, Alice's brother and Keith's sometime business partner. As these two men would leave their marks on Beaumont's future, so would Alice Carroll Keith, who as a young Beaumont society matron in the 1890s would establish a tradition of philanthropy that lasted until her death in 1956.

In 1870 the partners in Long and Company dispersed their interests among their family. The parent company, retaining its old name, began operating its huge plant as a shingle mill, which "turn[ed] out shingles like snowflakes," as many as 200,000 per day. Six years later, Joseph and Frank Carroll and J. Frank Keith built the Beaumont Lumber Company on the river just east of the foot of Main Street and opposite the courthouse; the mill eventually reached a capacity of 50 million feet of lumber per year. Still later, another of Long's sons-in-law, W.A. Fletcher,

---

Above
John Henry Kirby began his career in the Beaumont area by building the Gulf, Beaumont, and Kansas City railroad line in 1896. Immediately after the turn of the century, he bought heavily into the lumber business in Beaumont and rapidly expanded his interests throughout the region. Courtesy, Kirby Forest Products Company.

Above
There would be no lumber business without carpenters. A group of Beaumont's artisans posed with their boss about the turn of the century. Four of the men are known to be Jim Ory, Ed Van Wormer, Bart Wilkerson, and Simpson B. Stevenson. Courtesy, Tyrrell Historical Library.

joined in ownership by his brothers, Valentine and William, tore down the old mill in 1877 and built a new one complete with every imaginable innovation, including automatic slab carriers, cylinder or shotgun feeds, and a steam dry kiln, which ultimately increased its production from 5,000 to 100,000 feet of lumber per day in the 1880s. The mill was sold again in 1902 to lumber magnate John Henry Kirby.

The mammoth Centennial Mill, built in 1876 on the site of the old steam mill square by S.C. Olive and J.A. Sternenberg, was, in the words of an 1881 journalist, "extensive indeed and employing more machinery, we thought, than any other in the city—making lumber, shingles, etc., and also running planers." After Olive and Sternenberg built a new mill in Hardin County in order to be nearer the source of timber, the Centennial was sold in 1883, dismantled, and subsequently reassembled in Tyler County.

The Globe Planing Mill, owned by J.L. Williams, was not in competition with the other mills. It turned out finished products such as pickets, moulding, sashes, and doors. According to the correspondent from the *Orange Tribune,* "By working [the raw lumber] into finer material, [the planning mill] enhances its value, and thus retains and turns loose in Beaumont an average of $100 daily, which, without it, would go elsewhere."

Besides these major mills several smaller ones flourished during the last two decades of the 19th century. In 1880 Beaumont mills exported 26 million feet of rough lumber, 15 million feet of dressed lumber, and nearly 37.5 million shingles. Sawdust covered the town, clogging the ditches and rotting where it lay. Men worked in the mill from dawn until dusk, their universe governed by the scream of the steam whistle. One correspondent viewed the town in terms of its lumber: "Beaumont, for the most part,

bought the thriving riverfront Eagle Mill on the north side of Hickory Street from George W. Smyth, Jr. and Elias Seale, renaming it the Texas Tram and Lumber Company. Fletcher claimed that it was one of the largest and most complete mills west of the Mississippi River. A contemporary newspaperman remarked upon seeing the Texas Tram Company that it "was almost concealed from view by the piles of lumber stacked on its yard and ready for the cars."

Otto Ruff's mill, built in 1856 on Brake's Bayou, just south of Long and Company, was purchased by Harry W. Potter and Simon Wiess's son Colonel Mark Wiess, who named it the Reliance Lumber Company. Mark, later

Top
Long and Company maintained not only the usual company store but a company school for the children of its employees. This school was one of the first of many private schools in Beaumont before the public school system evolved at the end of the century. Courtesy, Tyrrell Historical Library.

Above
The phenomenal growth of Beaumont's lumber industry brought a reporter and artist from Frank Leslie's Weekly *to the city in 1890. Among the drawings accompanying the article was this one depicting the sawing and hauling crews of the Carrolls' Texas Tram and Lumber Company. Courtesy, Betty Cuthrell.*

Above
This high-wheeled cart was one of the devices used to transport logs to the railroad. The log was suspended by one end under the axle while mules pulled the cart. Courtesy, Kirby Forest Products Company.

consists of great piles of lumber, sometimes in rows, sometimes in squares, sometimes scattered promiscuously about; rows of square wooden buildings for business houses, cottages here and there, sawmills, and long strings of timber-laden cars.''

Beaumont was much more than a lumber town, however, both in its appearance and in the diversity of its industry. It actually had a broad economic base, all components of which were aided by the coming of the railroads. Cotton was still a substantial crop, although lumber soon surpassed it as the chief moneymaker. Shipments of cotton were exported from Beaumont both by rail and water, but increasingly by rail as cotton growers found that it was faster and cheaper.

Even though it was gradually overshadowed by some of the newer industries, Beaumont's early business of cattle-raising still constituted an important part of her economy and that of the surrounding area. Longtime cattleman William McFaddin, with his son William Perry Herring McFaddin, Valentine Wiess, and Dr. Obadiah Kyle, formed

an organization in 1888 called the Beaumont Pasture Company, a ranching concern located south of Beaumont and consisting of 60,000 acres of enclosed pasture land stocked with cattle. The Beaumont Pasture Company, in an attempt to improve its livestock, crossed the base breed with Herefords, which were good beef cattle, and with a Brahma bull (reputedly bought by the McFaddins from a circus), which was a hardy strain. The venture was successful, and soon the hybrid cattle were being shipped everywhere. At one point, several New York restaurants advertised "McFaddin steaks.''

William McFaddin did not confine his investments to the Beaumont Pasture Company; by the time of his death in 1897, he had built a ranching empire. His son Perry McFaddin followed in his footsteps, doubling his family's holdings and diversifying his interest to include rice farming, rice milling, meat packing, fur trapping, and commercial real estate. Like his father, he cherished a lifelong passion for land, once saying that he didn't want much—only what was his, and what lay next to it.

Above
Lewis M. Williams was foreman of a lumber loading crew at Sabine Pass in the days when Beaumont was inaccessible to lumber schooners. His wife, Ada, was the daughter of pioneer minister and educator Woodson Pipkin. Mr. Williams later worked as foreman of several dock crews in Beaumont. Courtesy, Fayetta Donovan.

Facing page
The first large-scale commercial rice milling in Beaumont began when Joe E. Broussard bought a grist mill in 1892. Broussard converted the mill into the Beaumont Rice Mills. Courtesy, Business Men's Studio.

The comparatively new rice industry also flourished during the last part of the 19th century. The *Beaumont Lumberman* in 1878 reported that John Jay French had shipped five barrels of rice to Houston. Since 1863, when rice was first grown for commercial purposes, its importance in Jefferson County had grown slowly but steadily. A local journalist in 1881 observed that "Rice is the crop for this country. The soil is well adapted to its culture, and all who have tried, have found it yielded as well as the same product does anywhere." In 1892 Joe Eloi Broussard, a Louisiana Acadian, bought a one-third interest in Price, Nash, and Company, a working gristmill, and converted it into the Beaumont Rice Mill, the first commercial rice mill in Texas. (Broussard was also a pioneer in the irrigation of rice, a procedure not practiced before his time.) Even though at the time of the mill's creation no more than a few thousand acres of rice grew in Texas, the crop soon became firmly established in the area. Only lumber was a greater money-maker.

In spite of the railroads and their great boost to transportation, Beaumont still depended heavily upon its original resource: the Neches River. Logs were rafted down the river to the mills at Beaumont and Sabine Pass, and the *Beaumont Lumberman* faithfully reported the arrival of the timber at high water:

The Neches River has risen. This is the highest rise at this season for several years. Pine still continues to come down in large lots. Over 5,000 logs were taken by the mills the first week of the rise and that is not half of the number this rise will bring down.

Ironically, the river steamers enjoyed a brief heyday just before they disappeared forever from the rivers of Texas. Their captains, absolute masters of their floating realms, were glamorous figures who brought the latest trinkets from Galveston, New Orleans, or New York, and the latest news from the outside world. Captains William E. Rogers, E.I. Kellie of Jasper, W.A. Fletcher, William and Napoleon Wiess, Cave Johnson, and Andrew F. Smyth of Bevilport, some of whom owned stores in their home ports, became legends in their own time.

One of the last but perhaps the finest of the steamboats to travel the Neches was the sternwheeler *Laura.* Bought by Captain Andrew F. Smyth in 1871 in Evansville, Indiana, for the unheard-of price of $11,000, the *Laura* was the most elegant sight on the river. Painted a sparkling white, she was 115 feet long with a 32-foot beam and two levels of decks. The upper deck contained 10 passenger cabins and a well-appointed saloon, equipped with a mahogany sideboard, a square grand piano, sofas, pictures, and mirrors.

The *Laura* made her first official voyage from Bevilport to Sabine Pass with a cargo of cotton in January 1872, thereafter steaming regularly up and down the Neches. On March 25, 1875, the *Galveston Weekly News* reported a typical trip: "The steamer *Laura* . . . left Beaumont today for upriver with 800 barrels of freight and numerous passengers. She will probably clear up the cotton for the present season on her return." Even after Smyth's death in 1879, the *Laura* plied the Neches under a new captain until the 1890s, when she sank near Beaumont. For many years her smokestack protruded above the muddy waters of the Neches, mute testimony to a vanished era.

As railroads preempted riverboat trade more and more, Southeast Texans' thoughts once more turned to the idea of utilizing the 60-foot depth of the Neches at Beaumont to create a major seaport there. In 1876, after conducting a survey of the Sabine-Neches water system, the federal government granted a large sum of money for the digging of a channel five feet deep and 50 feet wide through those ancient obstacles, the bars at the mouths of Sabine Lake and the Neches River. This project, which was begun in 1878, had the vigorous support both of Beaumonters and of citizens of the surrounding area, for it represented a vital step in the future of the Sabine and Neches rivers as shipping centers.

Before the results of the lumber boom began to manifest themselves, Beaumont retained many vestiges of the frontier. Unpaved streets were beds of dust in dry weather and seas of mud during the torrential rains common to Southeast Texas. Citizens frequently made use of ingenious mud sleds, pulled by oxen, mules, or horses. As one historian put it, "Getting to and from Beaumont was easier than getting around in Beaumont during inclement weather." Although mill owners J.M. Long and F.L. Carroll had white-painted houses of finished lumber, most Beaumonters' homes around 1872 were still of log construction. Yards were filled with kitchen gardens and livestock rather than lawns and shrubs. The paper complained of a flea epidemic in town "bad enough to make a statue lively."

A rapidly growing Beaumont also periodically found itself the host of a disruptive transient element. The town was the natural spot for journey's-end recreation for recently paid lumbermen, railroad workers, and riverboat men, who sometimes used firearms to punctuate their revels. In the words of one old settler, "In those days, if you

Above
Acting for a group of investors, Captain Andrew F. Smyth bought the Laura *(top) for $11,000 in Evansville, Indiana, in 1871. She was the finest boat on the Neches River, with a capacity of 600 bales of cotton, along with other freight. Cabins and a saloon were luxury items available to her passengers. Courtesy, Esther Walker.*

heard what sounded like shots from a gun, that's what it was.'' Between 1877 and 1881 the number of saloons grew from three to eight, largely in response to this added element. In 1877, the *Lumberman* reported with some trepidation:

> *Drunkenness has been quite common in our town for the past week. The depressing tendency of the weather and the loss of numerous logs caused a downward flow of spirits, which has led to a great many ups and downs, and the worst of it was that many of the downs were not able to get themselves up. We are pleased to say that those who have been participating in this*

debasing habit are not the citizens of our town and county . . . .

As a result of its thriving commerce, however, the face and character of Beaumont began to change. Although still an active sawmill town, it began to assume some of the trappings of its new wealth and to be conscious of its own possibilities. In 1876 Pearl Street was cleared and plowed, giving the town another main thoroughfare. A correspondent in Beaumont from the *Galveston Daily News* remarked in 1878, "[Beaumont] is a pleasing little place to the eye, on account of a wealth of green foliage, its stately oaks and sweet gums, and the general neat and tasty arrangement about

Above
The mud-sled or scow enabled grocer C.B. Chenault to make deliveries in spite of Beaumont's typically muddy streets. The house in the background belonged to Valentine Wiess and the building to the right was a power station. Courtesy, First United Methodist Church.

the yards of the citizens. There is some effort toward the cultivation of the beautiful about the homes. . . .''

In 1879 Beaumont acquired one of its landmarks: the Crosby House, named for J.T. Crosby, the president of the T&NO Railroad, and located opposite the depot. It proudly boasted a dining room, a ladies' parlor, five bedrooms on the first floor, and 12 on the second. The year 1888 saw the construction of a new three-story Crosby House, a building with a broad gallery, which in the evenings became the gathering place for the men of the town.

After the Civil War, George W. O'Brien had founded a small paper in Beaumont, the *Neches Valley News*, combining it in 1872 with the *Sabine Pass Beacon*, run by W.F. McClanahan, to form the *Beaumont News-Beacon*, its motto, "We paddle our own canoe." In 1876 O'Brien sold his paper, presses and all, to the editor of the *Beaumont Lumberman*, repossessing it when the *Lumberman* folded its tents.

MINERAL WATERS, —FROM— THE CELEBRATED SOUR SPRINGS, NEAR BEAUMONT, TEXAS

Having procured the Sole Agency for the sale of these

HEALTH GIVING WATERS,

I will constantly keep on hand a supply ready for seipment.

The beneficial effects and curative properties of these waters, in cases of Dyspepsia, Chronic Diarrhœa, Loss of Appetite, General Debility, and all Cutaneous and Eruptive Diseases, have already established for them a high reputation wherever known.

To those who live at a distance, and desire to avail themselves of the benefits to be derived from the use of these celebrated waters, medicated by nature, I will take pleasure in furnishing (upon application by letter), circulars containing an analysis and full instructions necessary to their use.

Put up in Barrels, Half Barrels and Ten Gallon Kegs.

Address   MARK WIESS, Beaumont, Texas.

Frederickson & Harte, 139 Canal street, New Orleans Agents.

In 1880 O'Brien again sold the press and its accompanying equipment, this time to John W. Leonard, a young newspaperman from Melbourne, Australia, who had been a correspondent for a French newspaper, then for the *Arizona Daily Enterprise*, before coming to Beaumont to practice law. On Sunday, November 7, 1880, Leonard, with the assistance of his brother-in-law, Thomas A. Lamb, an Englishman from India, brought out the first issue of the *Beaumont Enterprise*, an institution which has catalogued the growth of the town to the present day. The *Enterprise* was an outgrowth of several other short-lived area newspapers and was named for Leonard's previous Arizona employer. The paper was accompanied with this apologia: "The new devil set this up, and if you do not like my typesetting, you can get someone else—and don't you forget it!''

In 1881 the Texas legislature passed an act stating that a town with over 1,000 inhabitants could be incorporated if it so desired. John Leonard, through the *Enterprise*, urged incorporation for Beaumont:

As matters stand now we have neither good order, decent roads nor any semblance of sanitary arrangements. If a vagrant chooses to get drunk and take a siesta on the sidewalk where ladies have to pass, he does so undisturbed. If a party of wild boys wish to make the night hideous by discharging pistols in the

---

Top
John B. Goodhue built the original Crosby House in 1879 to accommodate passengers on the Texas and New Orleans Railroad, of which he was vice-president. It was named for J.T. Crosby, president of the railroad. The wide veranda of the second Crosby House, shown here, served as a natural gathering place for Beaumonters. Courtesy, Business Men's Studio.

Above
The weekly Beaumont News-Beacon *continued the evolution of Beaumont newspapers. Two predecessors, the antebellum* Beaumont Banner *and the* Neches Valley News, *had not flourished. The city's current morning paper, the* Beaumont Enterprise, *was born in 1880, when George W. O'Brien sold the* News-Beacon's *equipment to John W. Leonard. Courtesy, Chilton O'Brien.*

Above
Readers of the Beaumont News-Beacon *in 1873 did not yet know the value of what was hidden below Spindletop. Long before the drilling commenced, merchant Mark Wiess profited from marketing the gas-laden liquids that bubbled up from Spindletop Springs. Courtesy, Chilton O'Brien.*

town, there is nobody to say them nay. If anybody wishes to obstruct a ditch, he does so without interference.

Leonard was vindicated; Beaumonters voted 115 to 107 for incorporation on July 12, 1881.

In its transition from frontier settlement to city, Beaumont began to acquire modern conveniences. Although muddy streets continued to be a problem until after the turn of the century, boardwalks laid in front of some businesses offered relief. The *Enterprise* pushed for more: "The approach to the Beaumont Academy is a slough of despond. Just a few hundred feet of plank walk would make a connection all over town. We hope the trustees will make some arrangements to have this matter fixed up." In matters muddy, however, Beaumont was still better off than Houston, according to the *Enterprise*: "Colonel Stewart is in town, and says the mud here is nothing compared to Houston mud. There you bog to the knees every step you take, and further, Beaumont is far ahead of Houston in plank walks."

While they were improving other aspects of their community, Beaumonters began to provide facilities for the growing number of cultural events taking place in town. Early theaters were the Blanchette Hall on the second floor of the Blanchette Store on Main Street and the Bluestein Hall, built in 1881 at the corner of Tevis and Forsythe. In 1883, just behind the Crosby House, Colonel A.F. Goodhue built a large frame building, called the Crosby Opera House, which became the new entertainment center for the community. Here Beaumonters were occasionally treated to a play given by a traveling stock company, but more often attended home-produced entertainment.

In 1889 a two-story brick structure called the Goodhue Opera House was erected next to the Crosby Opera House. This facility was on an established circuit, which brought shows to theaters between New Orleans and San Antonio, and which at times featured such stellar performers as Lionel Barrymore and Theodore Roberts. The organization of the Woman's Club in 1895 was also a great boost for the arts, as they imported musicians and artists of renown to appear in Beaumont under their auspices.

Despite such cultural strides, Beaumonters retained their enthusiasm for simple entertainment. Dancing continued to be a favorite form of recreation. In the 1880s the newly formed Beaumont Social Club announced a "grand reception and soirée dansante." Beaumont even hosted a precursor of the Neches River Festival called the "Grand

Above
This picture, taken circa 1885, shows the Crosby Opera House sandwiched between the Crosby House (right) and the J.B. Goodhue cottage. The opera house was Beaumont's amusement center, featuring professional guest artists as well as local amateurs. Courtesy, Richard Graf.

Top
Muddy streets did not deter the construction of substantial business buildings. The E.L. Wilson Hardware Company, built in 1892, included an office building, a warehouse, and a retail outlet. Courtesy, Tyrrell Historical Library.

Tournament and Strawberry Festival,'' sponsored by the Ladies' Guild, the Council of Temperance, and the trustees of Magnolia Cemetery. For amusement, there were jousting, sack and horse racing, and other sporting events, followed by the crowning of a Grand Knight and his Queen.

Picnic excursions were popular. On the day of the American Centennial of 1876, obliging T&NO officials loaded several flatcars full of picnickers and, to the accompaniment of the Beaumont Brass Band under the direction of J.E. Jirou, took the group 24 miles out of town for a peaceful picnic in a cool shady place. Several years later, a rowdier July Fourth celebration held in town inspired this comment from the *Enterprise*: "Fire crackers and roman candles were plentifully displayed on Friday night last, disturbing the citizens and placing the town in imminent danger of fire.''

Top
Judge Hal Greer's cottage is pictured in the 1890s. On January 18, 1895, Mrs. Greer met with several women to discuss the formation of a women's reading club. Her plan led to the formation of the Woman's Club of Beaumont. Courtesy, Tyrrell Historical Library.

Above
Charter members of the Woman's Club of Beaumont were Mrs. Hannah Lamb (right) and her daughter Mary, who participated in the planning with Mrs. Greer. The Lamb family were pioneers in the stationery and office supply business in Beaumont. Courtesy, Tyrrell Historical Library.

Because fire was an ever-present threat to the lumber-laden town, the Beaumont Fire Company Number One was organized in 1881, a Grand Firemen's Ball being held to benefit it on October 18 at the new Bluestein Hall. The gala affair was perhaps too much of a success, for the following item appeared in the *Enterprise* a few days thereafter: "The members of the fire company were too much stove up by the ball on Tuesday night to attend the meeting on Wednesday. Meeting on Saturday, at 8 p.m. sharp."

When the state of Texas granted counties the right to hold local option elections on the question of drinking, Jefferson County did so in 1879. The "wets" so decisively defeated the "drys" that no more local option elections were held until well after the turn of the century. Defeated in their efforts to outlaw liquor, the Beaumont Temperance Council decided to offer citizens a genteel alternative to the saloons. On November 20, 1880, a reading club was organized; immediate plans were made to build a hall on the corner of Bowie and Pearl streets, on a site purchased for $100. Temperance Hall, as it was known, became not only a social center but a cultural one, for it held the town's first library.

During the early 1870s local education was still provided by private schools, even though they were supervised by trustees of the county. However, in 1879 a group of citizens organized the Beaumont Academy Company, subscribing $600 for a new building to be located on Park Street and selling shares to fellow Beaumonters at $5 each. George W. O'Brien was elected president of the board. In 1883 the Beaumont School District was organized, and the first graded school system began in 1884.

Black education also progressed. In 1870 the first for-

Above

Members of Beaumont's volunteer fire department, formed in 1881, paid 75 cents each for the privilege of serving. This pumper was operated by hand after being drawn to the scene of the fire by mules Kate and Roddy. Seated, from left to right, are Tom Galgish, George W. Carroll, and Ed Wilson; standing are Reuben Weber, W.A. Ivers, George Millard, Savinee Blanchette, W.J. Owens, and A.B. Doucette; on truck are Ed Ogden, Joe Reeves, Lee Wilbarger, Val Boyer, Van Petty, and Hank Solinsky. Courtesy, Beaumont Fire Department.

mal school for black children was held in a building near the courthouse. Later the school was moved to the upper floor of the home of the Reverend Woodson Pipkin, a black minister who was formerly slave and bodyguard to white Methodist minister John Fletcher Pipkin.

Charles Pole Charlton, a former slave, had arrived in 1869 in Beaumont from Woodville; a successful business-man, he had established a lumberyard and then branched out into other business ventures, including real estate. Together he and Pipkin organized a school for black children in 1874, where Charlton probably served as a volun-teer teacher. Pipkin and Charlton also helped organize a second school in the Live Oak Baptist Church about 1878. After the Beaumont School District was organized, all black children attended the Beaumont Colored School in the north end of town, under the tutelage of T.T. Pollard.

By 1880 denominations had finally appeared in Beau-mont religion. Since the days of the Alligator Circuit and John Fletcher Pipkin's brush arbor meetings, a Methodist church building had been constructed in 1877 on South Street, which served both Baptists and Methodists and, after 1881, Presbyterians.

The Catholic Church first celebrated Mass in private homes. In 1879 Father Vitalus Quinon had built St. Louis Catholic Church, a frame structure located on the corner of Bowie and Orleans. A Catholic school also met in the church building. In 1894 a small group of Sisters of Charity of the Incarnate Word established Hotel Dieu, a three-story frame hospital with space for 24 patients. The hospital was located on the banks of the Neches a few hundred yards downriver from Cave Johnson's live oak, now known as the O'Brien Oak because of its proximity to George W. O'Brien's stately home at the bend of the river.

In May 1895 the St. Louis Church was moved to the square block bounded by Forsythe, Jefferson, Wall, and Ar-chie streets. In 1903 the cornerstone was laid for a new church, which was completed in 1907 and dedicated to St. Anthony of Padua.

Above
T.T. Pollard, after some training from Tuskegee Institute, began his long career as a Beaumont educator in the late 1880s. The names of two pioneers in local black education were honored in the naming of Charlton-Pollard High School in 1925. Courtesy, Tyrrell Historical Library.

Above
Charles Charlton, ex-slave from Tyler County, shared the organizing of the first black schools in Beaumont with Woodson Pipkin. Classes were held in various buildings, including the Live Oak Baptist Church. Courtesy, Tyrrell Historical Library.

The earliest Jewish services were conducted by lay leaders, either in private homes or in the Bluestein Hall or Crosby Opera House. The Jewish community in Beaumont actually dated from the brief sojourn in 1838 of Polish native Simon Wiess, who soon forsook his native religion, becoming, like his wife, a Presbyterian. In 1878 Morris J. Loeb, the first practicing member of the Jewish faith, brought his family to Beaumont to open a cigar store. In 1881 the *New Orleans Times-Democrat* declared, "Seven new stores have been built in Beaumont in the past forty days and a number of Israelite merchants have settled here, a sure precursor of the prosperity which is to follow."

The Jewish community proved indeed to be an asset to Beaumont. Leon R. Levy, a member of the committee that raised $20,000 to aid hurricane-damaged Sabine Pass, served on the board of the First National Bank for a time during the 1890s. In 1889 Hyman Asher Perlstein came to Beaumont with $11.90 in his pocket, going to work for a blacksmith for 50 cents a day and eventually buying out his employer. After profiting from the Spindletop boom, he built Beaumont's first skyscraper in 1907, which at that time was the tallest building between Houston and New Orleans; from then until his death, he remained a business and civic leader.

Above
The St. Louis Catholic Church (top) was originally built at Orleans and Bowie in 1879 under the leadership of Father V. Quinon. The Church was moved to Jefferson Street between Forsythe and Wall in 1894; the convent was completed by 1900. Courtesy, Tyrrell Historical Library.

Above
Twenty-year-old Hyman Asher Perlstein arrived in Beaumont in 1889 and received a job at this blacksmith shop at Pearl and Fannin. He soon bought the shop from his saved earnings of $250 and expanded into the selling of farm implements, buggies, and Studebaker wagons. He progressed rapidly in business and real estate and built Beaumont's first skyscraper in 1907. Courtesy, Tyrrell Historical Library.

The decade of the 1890s saw many new Jewish arrivals: Jake J. Nathan, Jake Sharfstein, Louis Mayer, Bernard Deutser, Joe and Leon Rosenthal, all merchandisers; E. Szafir, a stationer, and others. Nathan became one of the town's leading citizens, donating generously to every worthy cause, including practically every church in town, regardless of denomination.

The ethnic makeup of Beaumont, for so long predominantly Anglo, Acadian, and black, was being diversified by other new groups besides the Jews. Compelled to leave their homeland because of unfavorable economic conditions, many natives of Sicily, including the Liberto, Rinando, Fertitta, and Serafino families, made their way to Beaumont after 1879. A frugal, hard-working, self-sufficient people, the majority were farmers, although many worked for the sawmills (making about a dollar a day), saving what they could to open small stores. In April 1905 Sam Maida, Frank Liberto, Joseph Caliano, and Nick Lamont formed the committee which founded St. Joseph's Catholic Church, a national diocese established directly by the Vatican. Since the church offered services in Italian, most Sicilian Catholics attended St. Joseph's until well into the 20th century. The early immigrants were soon joined by others, the Daleo, Lovoi, Brocato, Coco, Luparello, Serio, and Busceme families, to form a sizable Sicilian community in Beaumont.

As a result of the potato famine in Ireland from 1845 to 1847, Beaumont eventually gained another productive group of people, some of whose fellow countrymen, such as the O'Briens and the McFaddins, had been gracing South-

Above
One of Beaumont's early Greek immigrants, George Gielis, opened the O.K. Bakery at 810 College Street. Nineteenth-century Greek immigrants often ran small food distribution businesses. Courtesy, Tyrrell Historical Library.

east Texas for several generations. Irish native Margaret McDade Cunningham, the widow of Irish coal miner John Cunningham who had immigrated to America in the mid-19th century, brought her daughters, Eleanor and Johanna, to Beaumont in 1905. Eleanor married David Redmond Barry, who had come from an Irish colony in Louisiana after Spindletop erupted, to live and work in Beaumont. Johanna married John Henry Phelan, an Irish grocery salesman who was to make his fortune in the second Spindletop boom. He and his descendants would figure prominently in the subsequent history of the town.

The first natives of Greece to come to Beaumont were John and Aphrodite Carabin, who came to live with Carabin's uncle in Galveston just before the 1900 storm there. Surviving it, but possibly wishing to live a little farther inland, Carabin moved to Beaumont in 1906, where he became a railroad workman. Shortly after the arrival of the Carabins, brothers John and Harry Yianitsas moved to Beaumont, followed in 1910 by Pete Cokinos, the progenitor of an outstanding Beaumont family, one of whom, Jimmie P. Cokinos, served as mayor of Beaumont from 1956 to 1960.

When Arthur Stillwell built the Kansas City Southern Railroad, he obtained financing from Dutch bankers in Amsterdam, Holland. Many Dutch families, hearing of the project through Dutch colonization companies, immigrated to the United States, some to work on the railroad, some to farm. The first Dutch settler to arrive was Gatze Jans Rienstra, who came to Beaumont in July 1897, where he farmed and worked as a blacksmith. Pleased with the area, he praised it to Stillwell's agent in Holland, his enthusiasm encouraging other Dutch families to follow him. They

Above and right
The W.W. Kyle home, built in 1898, is a product of turn-of-the-century prosperity in Beaumont. Finely carved Louisiana cypress adorned both its interior and its exterior, and the custom-pressed brick was from St. Louis. Courtesy, Walter Sutton. Carved wood photo by Wesley Norton. Courtesy, Spindletop Museum.

rapidly and steadily, particularly after its ship channel was dug to the Gulf in 1899. Joseph Grigsby's colony of Grigsby's Bluff became Port Neches soon after the turn of the century. Orange, which was first called Green's Bluff, then Madison when it became the county seat of the new Orange County (formed from the eastern half of Jefferson County in 1852),

named their settlement "Nederland," after their mother country. By 1898 approximately 100 Dutch immigrants had moved to Nederland, including the Doornbos, Koelemay, Ballast, Bruinsma, Terwey, Westerterp, Van der Weg and Gerbans families.

Other towns, some old and some new, were flourishing around the town of Beaumont during the last part of the 19th century. The old settlement of Sabine Pass, severely damaged by the hurricane of 1886, did not immediately recover; consequently, it was soon overtaken and surpassed by Stillwell's new town of Port Arthur, which was growing

Above and right
Robert W. Sanders, one of Beaumont's finest craftsmen, lavished attention on the building of his own home at 479 Pine Street just before the turn of the century. The house, featuring intricate woodwork inside and out and a self-supporting circular mahogany staircase, is being restored by owner Alan McNeill. Courtesy Walter Sutton.

was renamed Orange in 1858. During this time Beaumont, Port Arthur, and Orange began to establish an economic interdependency that in the future would prove vital to the prosperity of the entire area.

Beaumont at the turn of the century bore little resemblance to the frontier settlement of the 1850s. Now giant sawmills hugged the banks of the Neches, saws whining, stacks belching smoke, and masses of newly cut lumber being readied for shipment by rail or water to all points on the map. Within the town itself, wealthy citizens were building gracious homes on Sabine Pass Avenue, Pearl Street, Liberty Avenue, and particularly on Calder Avenue.

The general prosperity had brought modern amenities to Beaumonters, such as a telephone switchboard, which not only provided instant communication but extremely personal service (people generally asked the operator for their party by name rather than by number). The volunteer fire department now possessed firefighting apparatus. The Beaumont Ice, Power, and Refrigeration Company provided an electric light system to many downtown businesses. According to ads in the newspapers, Beaumonters were enjoying ready-made clothes, imported cognac, Havana cigars, fine colognes, and celluloid cuffs. In the words of a turn-of-the-century resident, "Beaumont was taking on town ways."

In the face of progress, some things would pass away. Nancy Tevis Hutchinson, who had seen so much of Beaumont's history and had created so much of it herself, died in Beaumont in 1876 at the venerable age of 80. And old John Jay French, declaring that the country was getting too fast for him, packed a few of his personal and household belongings into a horse-drawn wagon in 1884 and, taking his wife Sally but leaving behind his children and grandchildren, moved to Taylor County in West Texas, over 450 miles from the place that for so long had been his home. There his wife died in 1885, and he in 1889.

Although the past was disappearing, the future hung heavy with promise. Throughout the last three decades of the 19th century, small but insistent voices had continued to whisper of oil. Experimental drilling at Sour Lake in 1867 had produced a brief jet of oil and gas; a visiting doctor spoke in 1887 of a fine vein of oil under the sour springs at Beaumont. Soon these voices would no longer be denied. To those ready to listen, the land would give its richest gift. Then Beaumonters would face their greatest challenge: to utilize it well.

Above
Homer Chambers was one of several young men who became members of the Beaumont Light Guards when the Spanish-American War broke out. The unit drilled locally prior to May 1, 1898, after which it was mustered into service at Camp Mabry, Austin, with Chenault O'Brien as captain. The war ended before the unit saw combat. Courtesy, Ruth and Florence Chambers.

Chapter V

Spindletop: The Giant Under the Hill

I read carefully reports from the so-called geologists which discouraged me at first; however, I kept study-ing the geological formation in this section and in other states of America and soon decided that the geologists knew but little or nothing as to the origin and location of oil. . . .After careful study I decided that this section of the country was the greatest place on earth for oil and gas.

—*Pattillo Higgins, from the* Prospectus for Higgins Standard Oil Company, *1902.*

The new century opened in Beaumont with deceptive calm, the loudest voices coming from civic leaders determined to make municipal improvements commensurate with Beaumont's anticipated position as one of the largest cities in Texas. However, two cataclysmic events were soon to break the quiet.

The first was the great hurricane of September 8, 1900. Galveston, receiving the full force of the monster storm, was almost destroyed. Over 6,000 people died, and the dazed survivors found themselves amid the wreckage of their once-great city. Bolivar Peninsula, on the mainland near Galveston Island, was also hard hit, and many vacationing Beaumonters were trapped there as well as on the island for the duration of the storm. For weeks afterward the *Beaumont Journal* was filled with accounts of heroic acts and tragic experiences.

Olga and Alice Keith, daughters of Beaumont lumber magnate J. Frank Keith, were staying with their relatives, the Carrolls, in the Patton Hotel at Patton Beach (now Crystal Beach) while their parents were in New York. When the storm came, the hotel patrons took refuge in two sturdily built houses, the Carrolls going to one house and the Keith girls going to the other in the company of hotel manager Mrs. A.A. Irwin and hotel employee Tom Smith, known as Tom the Tramp. Mrs. Irwin reported that as the storm intensified, "We saw the house go piece by piece until only the dining room was left with all of us huddled there together." Determined to make her way to the other house,

Mrs. Irwin stepped out into the storm with Alice in her arms, holding Olga by the hand. The force of the wind and water immediately tore Olga away from Mrs. Irwin, and a huge wave washing over them rendered Alice unconscious. Believing her to be dead, Mrs. Irwin considered releasing her in order to save Olga, but "for some reason I could not let her go." At that point Tom the Tramp emerged from the house and, retrieving Olga from the roiling water and returning her to Mrs. Irwin, proceeded to revive Alice by rolling her back and forth over his shoulder. All managed to make their way back to the house, where the girls remained on a table above the water until the storm was over.

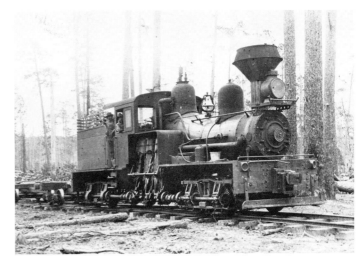

Facing page
"I set up my tripod about 250 feet from the well, on the side against the wind. I made the picture with an instantaneous exposure of one 100th of a second on a rapid speed dryplate." Thus was the most famous photo of the world's most famous oil well, the Lucas Gusher, taken by Frank Trost, Port Arthur photographer. Courtesy, Spindletop Museum.

Above
One of the decisive events of the 20th century was the coming of the automobile. Mr. and Mrs. John C. Ward ride in this electric Waverly, the first car ever in Beaumont and one of the very few in Texas in 1900. Courtesy, Business Men's Studio.

Top
Early Beaumont's handsome federal building and post office was completed in 1901 at the corner of Pearl and Bonham, costing only $75,000. This photo was taken in the 1930s shortly before its replacement. Courtesy, Business Men's Studio.

Above
Texas Tram Company's wood-burning Shay engine is shown in 1903 operating in Kirby Lumber Company holdings. The engine's driving mechanism consisted of gears designed to generate great power at low speeds. Courtesy, Kirby Forest Products Company.

C. VALENZUELA, Merchant Tailor

Suits pressed 50 cts.   Suits to order, $15.00 and up
Pants pressed 15 cts.   Pants to order, $3.50 and up

New Phone 518   716 Liberty Ave., next to Opera House

BEAUMONT, TEXAS

The distraught parents, who had read of their daughters' supposed drowning in a New York newspaper, were so grateful to find them safe that they not only offered a home to Mrs. Irwin but gave Tom a house at the company sawmill in nearby Voth. An epileptic, the tramp burned to death there in 1909 after kicking over a lamp during a seizure. The Keiths, in appreciation of his bravery, buried him in their family plot at Magnolia Cemetery. His tombstone reads: "Tom the Tramp: he alone is great, who by an act heroic, renders a real service."

Beaumonters, thankful that their city escaped severe damage from the killer hurricane, responded generously to Galveston's appeals for aid, sending a boat carrying ice and water to the city (it was reported to be the first to arrive) and beginning a relief fund for survivors, as did residents of many other Texas cities.

Even so, Galveston's tragedy presented to Beaumont an irresistible opportunity to advance its own fortunes. Less than two weeks after the storm, a *Journal* editorial posed the question: "Will Galveston rebuild?" The answer, at least to the editor, was of secondary importance, for even a rebuilt Galveston remained in constant danger from the vagaries of the weather. Beaumont, safely inland, could become the principal port for the Gulf Coast area merely by extending the already-existing Port Arthur ship channel northward to the city docks. As the *Journal* editor reasoned, "This is not suggested with the view of taking advantage of the awful misfortune which has overtaken Galveston, but it is presented merely as a business proposition which conditions will force to the notice and consideration of the great Trans-Mississippi country, as well as Congress."

As the possibility of a deepwater port became more

Above
In one of its first publications, the Chamber of Commerce featured Carlos Valenzuela's tailoring business on Liberty Street. Valenzuela employed at least a dozen men in the shop. Courtesy, Tyrrell Historical Library.

Above
George Douglas (standing) and T.L. Anderson made up the first graduating class of Pollard High School in 1901. The school was named for one of Beaumont's pioneer black educators, T.T. Pollard, who studied at Tuskegee Institute. Courtesy, Tyrrell Historical Library.

Beaumont Lumber Company, he had had a dangerous penchant for vandalistic pranks. One September night in 1881, after he and another man had set off a bomb outside a church and had shot out some of its windows, Higgins had a shootout with City Marshal W.E. Patterson. He fatally wounded the marshal and in return received a gunshot wound to his left wrist, which eventually necessitated amputation of his arm to the elbow. Tried for murder, Higgins was acquitted; however, his feelings of guilt and remorse weighed so heavily upon him that in 1883 he was converted to religion by a revivalist at the First Baptist Church. Always a man of extremes, he embraced his new religion with as much fervor as he had his previous misadventures.

It was at Spindletop, during picnics with the children's Sunday School class he taught, that Higgins began to real-

imminent, the feeling intensified among Beaumonters that the town was on the brink of spectacular growth. How spectacular that growth was to be, however, they could have no real idea. Less than five months after the hurricane, a second major event was drastically to redirect the economy of the entire area; south of town, men were drilling for oil on the low mound called Spindletop. When, centuries earlier, the Indians and the Spanish had caulked their boats with asphaltum from the beaches below Beaumont, they had foreshadowed fulfullment of a promise, the magnitude of which very few could yet comprehend.

A young Beaumonter named Pattillo Higgins had actually begun the search for oil years earlier in an investigation of fuels for his planned brick manufacturing business. A respected businessman, Higgins had a less than respectable past. As a young man working for George W. Carroll's

ize the Beaumont area might produce oil. In entertaining the children by showing them how a bamboo pole pushed into the ground released flammable gas, he became fascinated with the gas and with the unusual waters and muds of the sour springs. As he linked these phenomena with information gleaned from geology books, he concluded that, contrary to the belief of contemporary geologists who said the area had no oil reserves, there was indeed petroleum, and a great deal of it, under Spindletop.

Higgins' brick business never materialized, but by that time he cared only about finding oil. To obtain the necessary financial backing for his search, he approached George W. Carroll, his former employer and a member of his church. Carroll, excited by the prospect, consented to the scheme. "I think your idea is magnificent," he said, "I will be honored to join you." Higgins and Carroll included in

---

Above
Even before Spindletop, Pattillo Higgins analyzed the Beaumont economy, projecting its future in lumber and agriculture. Courtesy, Spindletop Museum.

Above
The family of F.L. Carroll, lumberman and capitalist of the 19th century, posed for this photograph in 1904. Left to right, standing, are sons George, Monroe, Will, and F.E. Carroll. Seated are daughters Minnie E. King (left) and Alice L. Keith (right). Carroll and his wife Sarah are seated in the center. Courtesy, First Baptist Church and Mrs. Ed E. Carroll.

the partnership George W. O'Brien and J.D. Lanier, both of whom owned land in the tract that Higgins wished to lease. On August 10, 1892, the Gladys City Oil, Gas and Manufacturing Company, named after a little girl in Higgins' Sunday School class, was formed.

The company never operated smoothly, principally because Higgins' feverish enthusiasm constantly conflicted with his partners' conservatism. When at last Carroll, O'Brien, and Lanier gave approval for drilling, the wells were abandoned (over Higgins' strenuous objections) before they reached oil sand because the primitive, flimsy equipment was inadequate to penetrate the hard rock which capped the hill.

By 1898 Higgins, deeply in debt and exasperated with his partners, sold his company stock back to Carroll, retaining only the land he owned on the hill. Carroll and O'Brien (Lanier had by this time also sold out to Carroll) still believed in Higgins but were reluctant to invest money in something so expensive and so elusive.

Undefeated but almost at the end of his resources, Higgins advertised, with Carroll's and O'Brien's approval, for a third party to finance drilling at Gladys City. Only one man ever answered Higgins' advertisement: Captain Anthony F. Lucas, an Austrian-born mining engineer who arrived in Beaumont in June 1899 to take over operations. Tall, striking, of military bearing, Lucas looked as though he could make history happen.

Having already done extensive salt mining in the Gulf Coast area, Lucas believed that many of the salt domes existing on the coast also contained sulphur, oil, or gas, and he knew that Spindletop was a salt dome. He leased 663 acres on its summit from the Gladys City Company and began drilling that same June. The well struck oil as planned, but only a small amount was brought in before the lightweight pipe collapsed from gas pressure. Lucas, like Higgins, was by now out of money; also like Higgins, however, he had no intention of giving up. The desire to find oil had now become an obsession. He took a small bottle of oil from the well and went East to seek help.

After being turned down by several promoters, Lucas presented his case to oil prospectors John H. Galey and James M. Guffey of Pittsburgh, who, convinced by Lucas' story, agreed to finance the well, in turn arranging their own financing with the Mellon interests, also of Pittsburgh. By the time Lucas had orchestrated the deal to everyone's satisfaction, he had leased almost 15,000 acres on and

Top
Drilling was a dirty, demanding, and often dangerous occupation. Boomers in 1901 worked amid pipes, steam, and mud at Spindletop. Courtesy, Business Men's Studio.

Middle
This early 20th century scene of the Port of Beaumont shows logs squared in local mills for shipment to Europe. To the right are the courthouse and the jail. Courtesy, William C. Gilbert, Jr.

Bottom
Rice farmers in 1910 utilized mules to pull the binder while a gasoline engine powered the cutting, elevating, and tying mechanisms. Courtesy, Texas A and M University Agricultural Research and Extension Center.

around the hill for the company of Guffey, Galey, and Lucas, retaining for himself only a small percentage of the anticipated profit. He was so intent on vindicating his conviction, however, that by that time his own interest hardly mattered to him. To underscore his faith in the project he refused even to take a salary for overseeing drilling of the well.

Guffey and Galey engaged a drilling firm operated by the Hamill brothers, an experienced team from the Corsicana, Texas, oil field. Two of the brothers, Al and Curt, arrived on the hill with their equipment, built a wooden derrick on the proposed well site from a pattern drawn upon the ground, and began drilling. From October 1900 to January 1901, the Hamills worked and Anthony Lucas watched, supervised, and prayed. The equipment actually was little better than that used by previous crews; the difference lay in the men who operated it. Inventive and resourceful, they proved to be the key that unlocked the mystery of Spindletop.

Slowly, and at times almost imperceptibly, the drill bit deeper, finally coming to rest in an oil sand which not only refused to give up its treasure but continually clogged the drilling pipe. The night of January 9, St. Elmo's fire, a phenomenon which had been seen many times in the vicinity, flickered across the top beams of the derrick. Lucas, seeing it, commented to his wife Caroline that sailors considered the eerie light to be a good omen.

On the cold, clear morning of January 10, as the perplexed and exhausted Hamills were installing a new bit, mud suddenly bubbled, gushed, then shot out of the drilling hole, pushing the four-inch pipe completely out of the well and scattering it around the derrick before ceasing as suddenly as it had begun. The Hamills were just beginning to resume breathing when mud and gas again erupted from the hole, followed by a geyser of blackish-green oil. This time it didn't stop.

Lucas, in town to obtain supplies for his men, was purchasing food at the French Market when a frantic roustabout, covered with oil, burst into the store, shouting, "Captain Lucas! Come quick—oil's shooting out of the ground and we can't stop it!" Lucas' horse was being shod; on a horse borrowed from Jim Blain, the owner of the French Market, Lucas galloped with all speed back to the hill to see for himself the wonder he had wrought. When he reached the well site, he beheld in amazement a towering plume of oil that shot over a hundred feet into the air, then dissipated

Nothing so momentous as the Lucas Gusher could escape the maw of popular culture. A pulp novel appeared in 1907 (above right), and local composers printed music and lyrics celebrating the "Lucas Geyser" (right). Courtesy Ethyl Corporation (book cover), Spindletop Museum (sheet music).

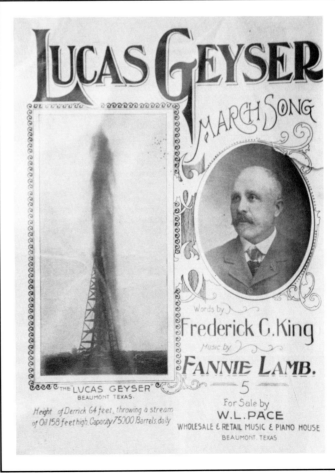

in the fresh north breeze to shower down upon the surrounding countryside.

Others had also seen the well when it blew, and soon everyone in town had heard the news, most going to the well to see for themselves. News of the phenomenon went out quickly from Beaumont by telephone and telegraph, and by evening the world knew of the momentous events taking place in the quiet little town in Southeast Texas.

The well spouted uncontrolled for nine days before the Hamill brothers were able to cap it. It soon became the Lucas Gusher, appropriately named by a workman frantically building a levee to contain the rapidly spreading oil.

Immediately after the well had come in, John Galey had warned that Spindletop must be proved to be a large field to justify a change of fuel from coal to oil by world industry. Proof was soon forthcoming; by April there were six gushers on the hill. Spindletop's production far outstripped the total yield of the rest of the world. Oil men, speculators, and promoters of every stamp rushed to Beaumont to make their fortunes, jamming the daily trains and pouring into the city by horse and buggy. Beaumont, already crowded with sightseers, quickly filled to capacity, then overflowed. In a short time the population jumped from its original 9,000 to over 50,000.

Every hotel in Beaumont was soon bursting at the seams; visitors, with nowhere to stay, milled about the congested streets. Men who could afford it often took the train to Houston in the evening and during the night rode the sleeper back to Beaumont, while many less prosperous individuals slept in the streets. Even chairs in hotel lobbies were rented for months in advance.

A citizens' meeting opened the city auditorium as a place of refuge. The ladies of the Christian Church sold coffee and sandwiches in the post office. Some enterprising townspeople, turning inconvenience to good account, rented rooms in their homes; others set up food tables in empty lots. Eventually the strain on the town's sanitation facilities brought on an epidemic of dysentery. The only alternative to contaminated water being whiskey, the Women's Christian Temperance Union (WCTU) tried to ward off the stampede to saloons by increasing their supply of free boiled water at stations along the streets. Other Beaumonters, not so altruistic, profited by selling the boiled water at a dollar a jug.

Crowds were thickest on the Crosby Hotel gallery, which was divided into small stalls used by various stock companies as offices. There speculation ran rampant in land and oil. Dr. George Parker, a young physician who, lured by rumors of fortunes to be made, arrived in Beaumont in the spring of 1901, described the scene:

Men and women, gesticulating wildly, ran from one stall to another. Stacks of green-backs stood out in vivid contrast against the blue of the maps. I had never seen so much money. I stood and watched with amazement as hundreds of thousands of dollars were exchanged for future oil wells in the Great Spindle-Top Oil Field, Texas' first gusher field.

Within a year of the gusher's advent, Beaumont had more than 500 oil and land corporations operating in town, the majority of them disreputable. Excursion companies made fortunes by bringing prospective buyers out to see "gushers," capped wells which were temporarily reopened by bogus stock company executives in order to make sales.

Above
Housewives reacted very quickly to the shortage of rooms, converting homes to boardinghouses to accommodate the boomers. This boardinghouse was one of two on Buford Street. Courtesy, Richard Graf.

Above
Stock certificates abounded after Spindletop came in, some of them of much greater value than others. This certificate, signed by George W. Carroll, was undoubtedly sound. Courtesy, First Baptist Church and Mrs. Ed E. Carroll.

In desperation, a group of citizens organized the Beaumont Oil Exchange, which recognized only legitimate companies and thus gave some measure of protection to those who sought it.

Beaumonters were not oblivious to the intrusion of potentially undesirable elements. The newspaper interspersed its oil news with editorial appeals for law and order and suggestions for putting the "floating population" to work on street improvement projects. Churches sponsored missions in the oil field, and ministers preached against the vice in town, as did the Reverend C.M. Davenport of the First Methodist Church who appealed to his congregation to save the young men from the saloons and gambling houses "with all their glitter and glare." The WCTU sponsored a temperance lecture in the city auditorium (after first fumigating it to rid it of unsavory reminders of the refugees who had recently slept there), while the Salvation Army set up its first permanent headquarters in town in February 1901.

However chaotic or uncomfortable life in Beaumont might have been, life in the oil field was much worse. Dr. Parker, in search of lodgings and unable to find them in town, traveled via horse-drawn hack from Beaumont out to Spindletop. As he headed south, the magnolia- and cape jasmine-lined streets, which took him to the edge of the city, soon became a single shell road, surrounded by flat saltgrass terrain. The trees along the road gave way to numerous saloons, which in their turn were replaced by derricks as the doctor entered the oil field.

Parker, renting a room at a drab, dirty hotel some-

where on Spindletop Hill, decided to visit the resident physician. In a dingy office he found a dissipated, middle-aged alcoholic who unexpectedly donated his practice to Parker by the simple process of leaving on a permanent drinking spree. Upon the older doctor's departure, Parker was immediately plunged into the turmoil of a boom town: the noise, the filth, the misery, the vice—and the excitement. Within a day after his arrival he had patched up a mangled oil field worker (for which service alone he received $20) and treated a baby for rickets. He had also visited several saloons and gambling houses, remarking on the appearances of the prostitutes who frequented them:

Old, haggard creatures with dyed hair, sensuous lips, and painted, wrinkled faces mingled with pretty young girls whose freshness had not yet hardened into a look of lust and greed.

Parker's attitude toward the Spindletop field was one of "mingled revolt and fascination." In the end, fascination (and the promise of wealth) prevailed, and he stayed for several months, working day and night and thus amassing quite a bit of money, treating oil field workers injured from working or brawling, attending prostitutes who attempted (or succeeded at) suicide, and assisting at an untold number of childbirths. The doctor never quite became reconciled to oil-field obstetrics, for many workmen's families were extremely deprived, and Parker felt it was a grim world that they entered:

The M.L. Hinchee house, built at 814 Park Street in 1901, was designed by the Hinchees themselves. Its interior is a prime example of Victorian furnishing. Mr. Hinchee, organist at First Baptist Church, kept this pipe organ in the music room (above), a room topped with a solid copper dome for purity of tone. Caroline (Gilbert) Hinchee painted the religious scenes on the walls and ceilings (above right). Courtesy, Ruth and Florence Chambers.

Sometimes the woman did not even have a shack to live in; many times it was a tent with a dirt floor in which she brought her young into the world. So many of the men drank and gambled, that their wives and babies were often without enough to eat and wear, to say nothing of having anything ready or sanitary for the new-born life.

At one memorable delivery in a dilapidated tent, Parker was accompanied in his efforts by the eloquent curses of the mother-to-be, directed both at her husband and at the doctor. When the baby finally arrived, the mother slept, and the doctor, a sporting man, rolled dice with the father, a terrified, drunken one, to see who, losing, would have to wash and dress the infant. Parker rolled high, but before he could escape looked up to see that the new mother had awakened:

She was looking in wild-eyed fury at both of us; then she burst out into a volley of the most torrid curses I had ever heard. The names she called us were beyond my comprehension as she told us where to go and what to do when we got there.

Parker bade the little family a hasty good night.

Later in 1901 a huge fire almost leveled the Spindletop field, at least for a time. During the ensuing recovery period, many of the drillers moved on, and the field became quiet. Dr. Parker found, somewhat to his own dismay, that he

actually missed the constant action. He left Beaumont, only to pursue his craving for excitement in Saratoga, Sour Lake, and other East Texas oil boom towns.

The frenzied activity at Spindletop that Parker had so vividly described attracted worldwide attention; at the same time, however, less publicized transactions were being made there that would have a lasting effect on the future of the oil industry. During the first year of the boom, three major oil companies were actually formed in Beaumont: Texaco, Gulf, and Humble (now Exxon). A fourth, Sun Oil Company, received the enormous push it needed to grow from a small company to a major one.

Standard Oil, which had a monopoly in the business from the beginning, drilled no wells in the Spindletop field. The company, approached for backing by both Higgins and Lucas, had declined because the area was not yet proved. This caution cost the company its stranglehold on the oil industry. Yet Standard was not to be left out entirely; in 1903, the year that Spindletop ceased to produce gushers and became a pumper field, Standard Oil interests built the Security Refinery nearby. Their timing was perfect. The need for a place to store and refine the accumulated crude oil had by then become critical, for the market that John Galey had declared to be so necessary for the survival of the petroleum industry was indeed developing with amazing rapidity. In 1907 a group of businessmen bought the Security plant and renamed it the Magnolia Refinery. It became the city's largest employer, and because it processed crude oil from many area fields made the demise of the orig-

Above
Gushers spawned refineries and tank farms. These two men with their mules and primitive equipment clear ground to build a tank farm at Magnolia Petroleum Company in 1909. Courtesy, Business Men's Studio.

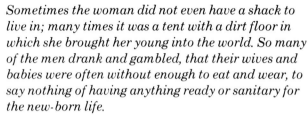

Above
Fires at Spindletop were very common and very well-attended. At one time the closely-set derricks in the Hogg-Swayne unit were completely destroyed by fire. So great was the zeal to find oil, however, that the field was restored in 10 days. Courtesy, Tyrrell Historical Library.

inal Spindletop field much less traumatic for the local economy.

Neither of the principals in the drama of Spindletop was involved in these historic developments. Pattillo Higgins, resentful that he had been excluded from the final Lucas-Guffey-Galey deal, sued both George W. Carroll and Anthony Lucas for what he believed to be his share of the profit. Even though Higgins received a favorable judgment in an out-of-court settlement, he never quite forgave Lucas, nor did he forgive Beaumonters for their initial lack of support of his beliefs. He soon moved on, finally settling permanently in San Antonio. Lucas, the man of science, unable to adjust to his loss of privacy and to the general disorder of post-gusher Beaumont, left Southeast Texas late in 1901 for Washington. Neither Higgins nor Lucas amassed the great personal fortunes from their discovery that others did; however, their dedication to the search for oil kept them in the business, both men using their considerable knowledge to realize greater profits later in their lives.

As the first frenzied year of the oil boom drew to a close, Beaumont began to return to normal, the permanent population stabilizing near 20,000. Most of the speculators, false stock promoters, and other shady entrepreneurs had by then gathered up their fortunes—or cut their losses—and left town; remaining newcomers were employed in legitimate occupations, many of them oil-related, in and around the city. The chaos had had its compensations; by July 1901 the number of banks in town had doubled from two to four, and total deposits had jumped from $661,818 at

the end of 1900 to $3 million. Beaumont thus returned to the business of growth and progress with a much larger city to serve but with a great deal more capital than it had had in 1900.

In 1902, $3 million worth of construction, much of it residential, was begun. The city also installed natural gas, developed an artesian water supply, and built a city hall, jail, and fire station. Several churches in town were able to construct new sanctuaries: the First Baptist Church congregation completed an architectural showplace in 1903. The population grew to 25,000 as new industries drew even more employees.

One outgrowth of the oil boom was a gradually strengthened prohibition movement. Before Spindletop, the doctrine of temperance in Beaumont had served more as an alternative to excessive drinking than as a driving force for prohibition. Liquor became a real problem for Beaumonters, however, as the number of saloons burgeoned during the boom; the city that had had 25 saloons in 1900 had 81 by 1903. Many of the saloons had gambling rooms in the back and brothels on the second floor. As the moral authority of temperance dwindled, the saloon keepers, unmolested, grew not only in numbers but in influence as their establishments achieved a certain dominance as social centers.

After the chaos of the oil boom calmed somewhat, prohibitionists attempted to regain their lost ground and determined to be more aggressive in the future. As a part of that effort, temperance leaders invited one of their national

Above
On July 19, 1907, this assembly witnessed the "driving of the golden spike," connecting the local Beaumont, Sour Lake, and Western Railroad with the Frisco system which reached into the wheat and cotton belts. Courtesy, Tyrrell Historical Library.

Above
In 1902 the city built this fine new fire station downtown, at the same time presenting Chief Ed E. Eastham with a new horse-drawn "fire buggy." By the time of this photo, taken in 1911, the fire department had added its first motorized vehicles. Courtesy, Tyrrell Historical Library.

zealots, Carrie Nation, to Beaumont in October 1902, where she addressed a very small audience. Afterward in the Gowlen saloon she accepted the offer of a drink from a man standing at the bar; however, the bartender refused to serve her, hastily moving all his breakables to safety because of Miss Nation's penchant for smashing bar equipment. His anxiety notwithstanding, the majority of Beaumonters apparently regarded Carrie Nation with amusement or indifference.

Prohibitionists gained unexpected support the next year, however, when in May 1903 Constable Will Reddick was shot by J.M. (Doc) Harris, co-owner of the Metropolitan Saloon on Bowie Street, while Reddick was at-

tempting to close it down one Sunday. Harris' first and second murder trials ended in mistrials and he returned to his business, but not before he had harmed the local liquor industry. Many citizens who had never been prohibitionists saw the incident as an issue not of morality but of law and order. In a mass meeting at the Kyle Opera House, Hal W. Greer, a local lawyer, declared that "New blood, new life, new enterprise, new investments are not coming to a community that allows its laws to be openly and systematically defied." An outgrowth of the meeting was the formation of the Citizens Law and Order League, a nonpolitical entity that acted as a watchdog over the saloon industry.

The year 1904 brought to national prominence a man

Above
The identifiable members of this group of first and second graders in 1911 are Gilbert Adams (first row, second from left), Hawthorne Broussard (first row, fourth from left), Nita Sanders (third row, sixth from left), Odette Robichau (back row, far left), and Cleo Tatum (back row, sixth from left).
Courtesy, Beaumont Heritage Society. Donor: Nita McKnight.

who was already a legend in Beaumont: George W. Carroll, as famous for his religious ideals, charitable endeavors, and prohibitionist sentiment as he was for his lumber and oil wealth. He had greatly increased his fortune through his interest in the Spindletop field but reportedly deplored the discovery because of the vice it brought with it. Legend has it that one evening in 1903 he disguised himself and thus easily gained entrance to the Ogden Saloon, where at the height of the gaming he climbed on a table and announced that everyone was under arrest. After a shocked silence, during which he was recognized, the saloon cleared completely. The visit served a dual purpose: Carroll proved to the police chief that he knew gambling houses operated openly in town, and saloon owners for a time were more careful about whom they admitted into their establishments.

In 1902 Carroll had run for governor of Texas on the

Prohibition ticket, and in 1904 the national Prohibition Party nominated him for Vice-President of the United States. The party made a poor showing both nationally and locally; in spite of their respect for Carroll, most Beaumonters did not yet wish to live in a dry community.

In December 1905 the temperance issue became heated once again when the small daughter of a local constable, a man whom the prohibitionists considered an ally, was attacked by a drunk. When the attacker received only a 50-year prison term, the bitter father drank himself into a frenzy, then armed himself and besieged the jail with the intention of killing the guilty man. During the melée, the unfortunate constable was killed by police.

This alcohol-related tragedy caused even greater num-

Top
W.W. Kyle built the Kyle Opera House in 1901 as a center for the performing arts, where sometimes as many as 45 shows were presented in a season. The first talking pictures in Beaumont were shown in the Kyle on February 11, 1926. The theater closed in January of 1929, live theater having been replaced largely by movies. Courtesy, Business Men's Studio and Janet Heard Robinson.

Middle left
The brawling boom period left many Beaumonters aghast at the violence associated with hard drinking. As seen by this campaign button, one of the town's most distinguished citizens, George W. Carroll, ran on the national ticket of the Prohibition Party in 1904. Courtesy, Spindletop Museum, First Baptist Church, and Mrs. Ed E. Carroll.

Middle right
Charles K. Hamilton brought this airplane into Beaumont in April 1910, less than a decade after Orville and Wilbur Wright flew at Kitty Hawk. It is believed to be the first plane flown in Beaumont. Courtesy, Mary (Crary) Anderson.

Bottom
In 1913, Mrs. Edna Swindell Crary, left, paid $25 to go aloft with the barnstorming Katherine Stinson. Miss Stinson was only the second woman pilot licensed in the United States, having paid for her lessons with prize money won playing the piano. Courtesy, Mary (Crary) Anderson.

bers of Beaumonters to feel that the apparent arrogance of local saloon owners had to be curbed; as a result, saloon laws became stricter and more stringently enforced. It became not only more difficult but less prestigious to run a saloon in the area, and between 1907 and 1916 the number of liquor licenses issued in Jefferson County dropped from 100 to 42.

Beaumont never became a center for the prohibition movement, however. In 1916, in the first wet-or-dry local option election held since 1879, the wets again won. Only when the Constitutional amendment declaring prohibition had been passed did Jefferson County vote liquor out, and even then, in a last defiant gesture, the voters assigned to the ballot box at the Beaumont city hall voted to remain wet by a two-to-one margin.

Beaumont's dream of a deepwater port, which the Galveston hurricane had brought within the realm of possibility, came true in 1908. With the help of Samuel Bronson Cooper, a Beaumonter in Congress, a canal with a depth of nine feet was dug in the Neches from Beaumont to the Port Arthur ship channel. The next phase was spearheaded by W.P. Hobby, then publisher of the *Enterprise* and later governor of Texas. In 1916 the channel was further deepened to 25 feet, and a turning basin was scooped out in the bend of the river. Meanwhile, local businessmen had developed dock facilities on the waterfront so the new port would have an industrial district. The Port of Beaumont was at last a reality.

In 1917 Beaumonters turned their attention to Europe,

in April of that year enthusiastically joining with the rest of the nation to fight the Great War against the "beastly Huns." The day war was declared, 500 men jammed the city hall, formed the First Texas Regiment of Municipal Reserves, and vowed to do anything they were asked, from serving home guard duty to raising food. At that meeting, District Judge E.A. McDowell expressed the collective sentiments of the people of Beaumont when he declared, "We are called upon to crush the Prussian autocracy and absolutism and damned be the American who is not ready to go."

For the first time in its history, Beaumont was designated a United States military post. About 150 members of Company M, Third Texas Infantry, were assigned to the city, camping in town between the courthouse and the Pearl Street wharf. Led by Captain W.O. Breedlove, the company held drills and forced marches, and for a time the downtown area rang with the sounds of taps and reveille.

The *Enterprise* and *Journal* promoted patriotism tirelessly with editorials and short commentaries. The editors declared: "America is not bluffing. . . . This country means business," jeering, "The kaiser is promising the German people he will be good after the war. But he is starting too late. There won't be any kaiser after the war." The city band staged special concerts in Keith Park: they played, and Beaumonters sang, popular war songs: "Goodbye, Ma— Goodbye, Pa," "There's a Long, Long Trail A-Winding," "Over There," and others. Schoolchildren substituted military-style drill for their usual physical education activity.

Above
This photo shows the city wharf at the Port of Beaumont in 1915 prior to the deepening of the channel to 25 feet. Among those who pushed the expansion were William P. Hobby, editor of the Beaumont Enterprise, *Representative Martin Dies, and Senator Joseph W. Bailey. Congressman Samuel Bronson Cooper was the key to the first expansion in 1908. Courtesy, Tyrrell Historical Library.*

Above
In celebration of the opening of the newly dredged waterway in 1908, a crowd greets the Nicaragua, *a Norwegian ship purchased by Captain William C. Tyrrell. It was the port's first locally owned commercial ship. Courtesy, Port of Beaumont.*

Top
The City of Beaumont *was launched here in 1918 as a part of the United States emergency ship-building program. Among those pictured are Frank Alvey, Mary (Crary) Anderson as a child, Mrs. N.N. Crary, Mrs. Will Alvey, and N.N. Crary, manager of the ship-yards. Courtesy, Peabody Maritime Museum. Donor: Mary (Crary) Anderson.*

Above
The Melton Bowie family operated this grocery early in the century. It was one of the largest black-owned businesses in town during a time of limited opportunity for black entrepreneurs. Courtesy, Tyrrell Historical Library. Donor: Ezekiel Dearon.

Everyone, adults and children alike, planted backyard victory gardens and rolled bandages.

As the months passed, Beaumont increased its greatest contribution to the war effort—the lives of its young men. Families who had sons in the service posted in their front windows a white flag bordered in red, on which appeared a blue star for each family member in the service. If the young man died, his blue star was replaced with a gold one. Quite a few local families retained as a war memento a white flag with at least one gold star on it.

When the war at last ended in November 1918, Beaumonters rejoiced, for more than just the cessation of hostilities; the town had been under a health ban since October 8 from a double epidemic of influenza and smallpox. All public places—movies, churches, schools, and meeting-houses—had been closed until further notice. On November 3, however, the ban had been lifted, and, relieved that the toll had been no greater (out of 20,000 cases of both diseases, 75 people had died), the community was more than ready to celebrate both the end of the epidemic and the coming of peace.

News of the armistice reached town at 2:45 a.m., November 11 (Beaumont time). Peace had been expected, so by prearrangement all the work whistles in town sounded simultaneously, and Mayor E.J. Diffenbacher forthwith declared a holiday. The newspaper headlines read, "Beaumont Goes Wild with Joy as Peace Comes." Pearl Street was jammed by 9:00 a.m. as cars full of cheering people drove through crowds staging impromptu parades and street dances. The *Enterprise* enthusiastically reported:

Above
Army and Navy units marched down Pearl Street in 1918 as World War I was about to end. Beaumonters had proudly over-subscribed their $1.9 million quota for Liberty Loans by $300,000. Courtesy, Business Men's Studio.

Thrilled by the spirit of the new-born day women just out of boudoirs and hair uncombed and men whom Pearl Stret [sic] had never seen except in careful attire stood by collarless and coatless and laughed and cried and cheered and embraced and kissed.

When all was again quiet, Beaumonters totaled their contributions to the war effort and found that they had bought $5.7 million in liberty bonds and almost one million dollars in thrift stamps, had donated $207,000 to the Red Cross, $15,000 to the Knights of Columbus and $5,000 to the Salvation Army, and had raised and sent a considerable amount of foodstuffs. On a more somber note, about 4,000 soldiers went to war from the Beaumont area, but several hundred never returned.

The town benefited economically from the war. Among other signs of progress, the government had established the long-desired shipyards in the area for wartime production. In May 1917 the *Enterprise* referred to the duration of the war as the "most prosperous era in the history of the city," citing as examples the flourishing shipyards, refineries operating beyond capacity, the expanding lumber business, and even the rice industry, which had enjoyed some recovery from a slack period in 1909.

It was time to look ahead. The economy was booming from wartime activity, the population had increased from the influx of new shipyard employees, and the resulting housing shortage promised further benefits to the building and lumber industries. Once again Beaumont seemed to be on the verge of fulfilling its potential.

Above
Mr. and Mrs. Frank Keith built Arbol Grande, one of Beaumont's showplaces, on Calder Avenue in 1902. On this occasion, young ladies from the YWCA were invited to swim in the pool.
Courtesy, Mrs. Jane Clark Owens.

Chapter VI

More Oil: The Giant Reawakens

Yount-Lee brought in big flowing well yesterday on
my Spindletop leases. Sitting on top of the world.
*   — Marrs McLean's telegram informing*
his father of the second oil discovery at
Spindletop on November 13, 1925.

Beaumonters enjoyed a brief Golden Age from 1920 to 1930. Since the 1901 oil boom, the city had developed a broad-based economy, ensuring a prosperity that reflected that of the national scene. Midway through the halcyon twenties, citizens were handed an unexpected bonus with the renewal of the city's most profitable resource: oil. Having received the land's ultimate gift, Beaumonters began culturally and economically to enrich the quality of their lives. It was well that they did, because that enrichment temporarily sustained them when national prosperity evaporated in the face of the Great Depression of the 1930s.

The year 1920 began the decade somewhat inauspiciously; in May a catastrophe was averted when the city stamped out a threatened epidemic of bubonic plague brought in by one of the ships docked at the Port of Beaumont. Beaumonters, responding immediately to the call for help, cleaned up rat-infested areas; more than 500 tons of trash were hauled to the dump in a single day. The city hired a professional rat catcher from New Orleans, not only paying him a handsome salary but also a bounty of 10 cents for each rat he caught. Citizens were also paid bounties for the rodents. Not surprisingly, 17,482 rats were trapped in a two-month period. Serum was imported for those few actually stricken with the disease; thus fatalities were held to a minimum.

After this unwelcome interruption, the city resumed its enjoyment of postwar economic growth. Beaumont's impor-

tance as a shipping center increased with improved railway connections and a port channel that in 1922 was deepened to 30 feet, while lumber, iron, steel, sulphur, brickmaking, and a host of other industries rounded out the economy. However, the underlying base for all local prosperity was, as it had been since 1901, petroleum. Magnolia Refinery continued to process oil from surrounding fields in Texas and Louisiana, while many of the city's businesses manufactured products necessary to the oil industry.

The old Spindletop field was assumed to be virtually drained by the 1920s; however, on November 13, 1925, history repeated itself. A drilling crew brought in an oil well at Spindletop, this time on the flanks of the original salt dome. Once again two visionary men had discovered oil where people believed none existed.

Marrs McLean, reared in Sherman, Texas, first saw Beaumont as a boy during the 1901 oil boom. As an adult he returned to the area, first raising cabbages and water-

Facing page
Police Chief Carl Kennedy poses with one of the moonshiners' stills confiscated during Prohibition. The boiler of this distinctive still was fired by sophisticated gas burners. Courtesy, Business Men's Studio.

Above
An economic mainstay of Beaumont since the first decade of the 20th century, the Magnolia Refinery was the largest of the Magnolia Company's four Texas refineries. In 1939 Magnolia employed 2,200 workers, covered 1,440 acres, loaded 125,000 barrel tankers, and produced 35,000 barrels of gasoline and 4,000 barrels of lubricating oil daily, as well as a large volume of other products. Courtesy, Business Men's Studio.

Above
Ships such as the four-masted W.J. Patterson brought goods through the Port of Beaumont even during 1920, the year of the bubonic plague. The port, deepened to 22 feet in 1922, was among the 10 leading ports in the United States in tonnage before the end of the decade. Courtesy, Tyrrell Historical Library.

melons at High Island, then moving to Beaumont to manage a theater, and finally fixing his restless interest on the oil business, in which he became moderately successful as a drilling promoter.

McLean as a child had had a fascination with Spindletop, which as he grew older had become a conviction that there was still oil under the hill, not on its summit, but on its flanks. However, the first wells he drilled to test his theory were dry holes, causing his backers to withdraw support. Undaunted, McLean was on the point of risking all of his own money to drill the wells himself when Frank Yount, his neighbor on Calder Avenue, offered his services.

Frank Yount, president and guiding genius of the Yount-Lee Oil Company, was known in Beaumont and the oil industry not only for his expertise but also his integrity. Beneath his exceptionally quiet manner lay a brilliance and dynamism that not only benefited his associates but had a deep and lasting effect on the entire community.

Yount, hailing originally from Arkansas, had dropped out of school at the age of nine when his father died. Throughout the ensuing years of hard work he not only learned to accept responsibility but developed a rare capacity for self-education, much as Pattillo Higgins had. Such were his powers of absorption that in a very short time he could become an expert on a subject simply by immersing himself in it.

Once wishing to purchase a violin for his daughter Mil-

dred but knowing nothing about the instrument, Yount enlisted the advice of an expert and read all available information on the subject. He soon developed a working knowledge of rare violins, subsequently purchased two Stradivari, and eventually assembled an extraordinary collection of fine violins and bows. A violin expert, Ernest N. Doring, said of Yount with some amazement, "... his conversation on the subject was that of the experienced connoisseur."

In 1915 Yount formed the Yount-Lee Oil Company, consisting of himself, his friend Harry Phelan, brothers William E. Lee and Thomas P. Lee, E.F. Woodward, and Talbot Rothwell, Tom Lee's son-in-law. (The Lee brothers and Woodward had previously been with Texaco but had left the company when it moved offices from Beaumont to New York.) Yount ran the company virtually alone, and principally because of his singular ability to find oil, the stockholders were content to leave things in his hands. Their faith was justified; by 1922 the company was valued at $2 million.

Yount had had particular success drilling wells on the flanks of salt domes along the Gulf Coast, and had for several years believed, as McLean had, that an untapped supply of oil lay under the sides of Spindletop Hill. As soon as Yount made known to McLean his willingness to handle the job, they quickly made an agreement and began drilling. The first well was a dry hole, but the second, the McFaddin No. 2, struck oil. A decorous announcement of the occasion was made over the public address system at the Fairgrounds, where hundreds of Beaumonters were attending the South Texas State Fair.

Above
A new forest of derricks, now made largely of steel, arose at Spindletop after 1925. Compared to the boom of 1901, the second Spindletop oil discovery came at a time of much greater demand for petroleum products and of greater discipline in the business. While this second boom was quieter, it produced extensive economic growth in downtown Beaumont. Courtesy, Business Men's Studio.

Above
Skilled workers manned the refineries and machine shops essential to the oil industry circa 1923. The diversity of the Beaumont work force and its interest in organization is indicated by the listing of 38 labor groups in the 1920 city directory. Courtesy, Business Men's Studio.

In contrast to the geyser of oil that had heralded the first Spindletop discovery, this smoothly flowing well was controlled from the beginning. Also missing was the frenzy of land speculation because Yount and McLean already controlled most of the productive areas; the remainder, and the land that McLean finally decided to lease out himself, was taken principally by major oil companies.

Wells, mess halls, and bunkhouses once again sprang up on the oil field, but this time without the company of saloons, brothels, or miserable shacks. Correspondingly, downtown Beaumont hosted none of the pandemonium that had followed in the wake of the Lucas gusher, for the oil industry had matured into big business since 1901. Nor was there a frantic search for a market for the oil; America had become oil-hungry in the 24-year interim.

Thus Beaumont's economic well-being was greatly enhanced by the new field, which flowed over 59 million barrels of oil in its first five years of production. Citizens were rightly enthusiastic about the wealth it would bring to the city. Business leaders had for several years pushed construction projects to alleviate a shortage of houses and commercial buildings, but after 1925, there was no need to push; total costs of building operations jumped that year from nearly $1.64 million to $5.25 million in 1927. Beaumont's skyline, already graced by Hotel Beaumont and the San Jacinto Building, blossomed further with the construction of the Young Men's Christian Association building, St. Therese Hospital, and two badly needed hotels, the La Salle and the 20-story Edson (built at a cost of $1.6 million).

Blocked to the east by the river and to the north and

Above
Looking east down Laurel, circa 1937, the Edson, the Beaumont, and the La Salle hotels spanned the business district. Left to right otherwise are the Goodhue Building, American National Bank, and the San Jacinto Building, all of which still grace the Beaumont skyline. Courtesy, Business Men's Studio.

south by lower income housing, developers wishing to build more expensive homes turned west in spite of low ground and poor accessibility, laying out at least 18 new subdivisions in the west end of town after 1925. Here many of the men who made fortunes in the second Spindletop oil boom built their beautiful homes.

To improve the quality of life in their city, Beaumonters passed major bond issues to finance improvements in streets, wharves, docks, police and fire departments, the fairgrounds, water, sewer, and garbage facilities, and to construct a municipal auditorium and an airport. All three public school districts, Beaumont, French, and South Park, constructed new schools in the twenties, as did the Catholic diocese. South Park took the greatest step forward, building a white high school, a black high school, and, in an innovative move, creating in 1923 a junior college on the top floor of the new South Park High School building.

In spite of doubts about its survival, South Park Junior College grew by leaps and bounds, enrolling more than 100 students its first semester and graduating 65 in 1927. Such success was a vindication for its creators, for many Beaumonters had felt that, for its own future, South Park would eventually be forced to consolidate with the Beaumont District. The growing young institution was proof positive that South Parkers could make it on their own.

In 1923 Captain W.C. Tyrrell, recognizing a vital need, donated to the city the old First Baptist Church Building for use as a public library. The founding of the Music Study Club in 1921, the Beaumont Music Commission in 1923, the Little Theater in 1925, and an amateur symphony orchestra in 1926 also reflected Beaumonters' heightened interest in culture and entertainment. The Kyle Theater continued to book outstanding stage shows, engaging such stellar personalities as John Philip Sousa, Galli-Curci, Lillian Russell, Lionel Barrymore, Enrico Caruso, Victor Herbert, Pavlova, and Ignace Paderewski; however, the Kyle ironically

Above
The proprietors of streetcars did not intend to compete with themselves, but rather used buses to extend and connect streetcar lines and to provide charter service for, among others, school athletes and band members. Beaumont High's football team is ready to board from the downtown high school building in 1929. Courtesy, Business Men's Studio.

Top right
Beaumont's city hall and auditorium, currently being transformed into a center for the performing arts, was completed in 1928. Douglas E. and F.W. Steinman designed the building along modified classical lines of the Corinthian order. The site on which it was built had once been Keith Park. Courtesy, Business Men's Studio.

Above
Members of the First Baptist Church had built this fine Gothic-style structure in 1903 following the first Spindletop boom. Captain William C. Tyrrell bought the building for $70,000 in 1923 and gave it to the residents of Beaumont to house a public library, thus preserving the building and creating a memorial to his wife Helen. One of Captain

Tyrrell's conditions was that service be extended to black patrons; hence, a branch was opened in the Charlton-Pollard High School and eventually in other schools. Courtesy, Tyrrell Historical Library.

assisted in its own decline by showing its first talking movie on February 11, 1926. On October 1, 1924, the Magnolia Refinery radio station, KFDM, broadcast its first program from the refinery cafeteria, a performance by the Magnolia band directed by Harry Cloud. So popular was the station that in 1929 it greatly increased its broadcasting power and moved to larger quarters.

In the midst of this golden decade, Beaumont hosted one dark interlude: the rise to power of the Ku Klux Klan. Between 1922 and 1924 this shadowy force completely controlled local politics and resisted all external efforts to remove it. Bearing only a nominal resemblance to the Klan of Reconstruction days, the local Klan was part of a national organization that proved to be an enormous commercial success for its original promoters, who received a generous percentage of each initiation fee. By 1924 the group boasted 4.5 million members nationwide. While purporting to stand for traditional values, particularly law and order,

the Klan's system of vigilante justice actually represented lawlessness in its ugliest form.

Organized in January 1921, the Beaumont Klan the following May tarred and feathered a local physician who had been twice indicted, but never tried, for abortion. The physician subsequently left town. A rash of tarrings and featherings, lashings, and even pistol whippings followed, directed principally against physicians suspected of being abortionists, bootleggers, and other violators of the Klan's moral code.

After several months of violence, the Klan began to balance its punishments with charitable acts, presumably to improve its image. Typical was a $75 donation to the Children's Welfare Committee, accompanied by a letter reading in part:

Its membership is composed of men of all walks of life, with warm hearts and pure principles, and an

Above
"Castle on the Neches," as residents called their county jail, was formidable enough to discourage lawbreakers of the 1920s, especially if they considered the public hangings held in its yard. The building was destroyed to make way for the new courthouse, completed in 1932, which included a jail in its upper floors. Courtesy, Business Men's Studio.

eagle eye upon the conduct of every man and woman in our fair city, and woe will come to the man who steps aside from the path of right, be Thou our witness, Almighty God.

Opposition to the Klan quickly organized, sharply dividing the community. Publisher Jim Mapes and editor Alfred Jones of the *Enterprise* were excoriated by Klan supporters for opposing the organization's activities. Members of the Rotary Club passed a resolution condemning the Klan; however, Judge Stephen M. King was ruled out of order for attempting similar action at a Kiwanis luncheon. Mayor Steinhagen, declaring the Klan to be "as bad as Bolshevism," investigated city offices for suspected Klan sympathizers; not surprisingly, none admitted to membership. Other leaders of the anti-Klan forces were attorney W.D. Gordon and District Judge E.A. McDowell. McDowell stated, in a most unjudicial address to a 1921 grand jury:

I don't want to kill anybody. But if ever one of those fellows (and I know a bunch of them) acts suspicious around me, I'm going to kill him. . . .

In spite of McDowell's exhortations, the grand jury, stymied by the secret nature of the Klan, returned no indictments.

In 1922 a citizens' committee circulated a petition to remove from office Jefferson County Sheriff Tom Garner, a suspected Klansman, charging him with violation of his oath of office by participation in a society that operated outside the law. The subsequent trial to determine Garner's guilt or innocence was a victory for Klan forces; Garner was removed from office only to be reinstated by a higher court. In the 1922 primaries, the so-called "Klan ticket" won all offices in the county, Tom Garner retaking the sheriff's office by a large margin.

Above
The power of the Ku Klux Klan was near its peak in 1922 when this parade drew the largest crowd ever assembled in Beaumont for such an event. The national founder of the Klan later spoke to an estimated 30,000 at Fair Park. A number of prominent Beaumonters provided support and even leadership as the Klan vigilantes made themselves guardians of "morality, Americanism, and racial purity." Courtesy, Tyrrell Historical Library.

Above
Stephen M. King, a judge in the Court of Civil Appeals, publicly opposed the Ku Klux Klan when it was very unpopular to do so. Courtesy, Dale Dowell.

For the next three or four years, the Klan grew virtually unchecked. During Garner's trial 801 new members were recruited, and 10,000 spectators attended a rally for him at Magnolia Park. An estimated 50,000 saw the sinister sheeted figures of the local Klan march in the group's first public parade. The final blow to the anti-Klan group was the death of Judge McDowell, who was replaced by a pro-Klan judge. The Klan again swept local elections in 1924.

Klan control was complete but short-lived. Opposition had served to solidify the movement; left to itself, it died from within. As often happened with the many fads and crazes of the twenties, people simply seemed to lose interest in it. The state organization deteriorated quickly after 1925, while the local Klan declined more slowly because so many political and civic leaders in its ranks gave it respectability. By the end of the decade, the Ku Klux Klan in Beaumont was a small fraternal organization, nothing more.

Occasional threats against blacks or black groups had seemed to satisfy the Klan's demand for white supremacy, possibly because of the low profile maintained by the black community during this era. Blacks represented the largest minority in town—about 25 percent of the local population—and the most disenfranchised. The only areas of black progress acceptable to whites were in education and standards of living. Although rigid segregation was somewhat tempered with paternalism, the position of blacks in Beaumont remained basically unchanged from Reconstruction to the late 1950s.

Beaumont blacks had of necessity created their own economic and social structure, establishing restaurants, groceries, recreational facilities, and labor and fraternal organizations, and living in black residential sections scattered throughout the city. Although the majority of local blacks were employed as laborers or domestics, the black community listed in the 1929 city directory a number of educators, nine doctors, five dentists, and one lawyer.

Above
The first black band in Beaumont, pictured circa 1930, was founded and directed by a Mr. Turner. The band not only played local concerts but accepted out-of-town engagements in cities such as Waco and Dallas. At the left rear with trombone is Chaney Ratcliff; at far
right, Alex Molett. Playing the snare drum is Shellie Molett, and far left, kneeling with trumpet, is Lewis Molett. A number of the men were employees of Magnolia Petroleum Company. Courtesy, Tyrrell Historical Library. Donor: Ezekiel Dearon.

A local chapter of the National Association for the Advancement of Colored People (NAACP) had been founded in 1918 by black community leaders Dr. E.S. Cravens and Dr. C.B. Charlton. The group had remained fairly quiet, however, because the NAACP magazine, *The Crisis*, had mistakenly located the lynching of a black at Beaumont instead of Tyler, and some white citizens were angry at the error. In 1920 C.B. Charlton had said, "We have a few good white people here who are against lynchings. . . . Our branch has never been stopped or asked to suspend business." In 1924, doubtless coinciding with the dominance of the Ku Klux Klan, the chapter was disbanded, and no further organizational efforts were made until 1930 when the group formed again.

One reason for the widespread popularity of the Klan was that it had seemed to promise a return to the old days. The 1920s were a golden era, but they were also a time for questioning of traditional values, and the resulting social change caused great concern among those who saw in it the impending triumph of evil over good.

Newspapers and movies not only chronicled signs of "decay" but seemed to some to promote it. The *Journal* chided that the most consistent drawing card for picture shows was a sign reading "for adults only," while the *Enterprise* carried a "College Humor" section liberally sprinkled with jokes of dubious taste.

The 18th amendment to the Constitution, outlawing the manufacture and sale of alcoholic beverages in the

MISS. E. H. LANIER MRS. E. B. GROGAN MRS. M. L. WILLIAMS
PROF. W. W. McCARTER MRS. C. L. SMITH MISS. T. G. BOYD
PROF. J. H. MARION PROF. A. L. PRICE PROF. V. W. M. YOUNG

United States, should have reassured moralists in Beaumont; instead, Prohibition brought its own problems. Drunkenness became the most common cause of arrest as people seemed to drink more than ever. Moonshiners, bootleggers, and smugglers swelled the ranks of lawbreakers, and confiscated liquor soon overloaded law enforcement buildings where it was stored. In May 1923, 18 stills and 100 gallons of whiskey were collected; at one point in 1924, agents were holding $25,000 worth of liquor at bootleg prices. The beleaguered U.S. Marshal in the area declared in 1925 that he believed 90 percent of local families had made home brew that summer.

Drinking habits of local families were not the only causes for concern among moralists. The divorce rate was climbing; in 1929, Beaumonters were appalled to find that Jefferson County had more divorces than the entire state of South Dakota, with only one-fifth of that state's population. Moreover, the new social order seemed to threaten not only the family unit but also parental authority. The *Enterprise* editor lamented:

A modern father trying to lay down the law to a flapper daughter or to a slick-haired son with a penchant for fast roadsters and a hip flask complex is one of the saddest sights on earth.

The flapper, symbol of the 1920s as the Gibson Girl had represented an earlier era, did indeed jolt the old-fashioned sensibilities, not only of her parents but also of most citizens of a previous generation, for her outlook on life sharply contrasted with that of the Victorians. Alice Flasdyck, newcomer to Beaumont in 1920, writing for the *Enterprise* under the nom-de-plume of Betty Browne, kept for several years a personal diary filled with fascinating glimpses of Beaumont in the early part of the decade. In it Browne profiled a girl dubbed Elizabeth whom she considered to be the quintessential flapper, calling her "typical as I could ever find of the 1921 girl of 17. . . ." Browne described Elizabeth's outlook on relations with the opposite sex:

"I figure it this way," she says, abandoning "The Lady of the Camellias" for a moment. "There's no harm in letting the boys kiss you if you really like 'em a little bit. I won't let anybody kiss me I don't really like. Men aren't any too perfect. I don't see why girls should be."

Elizabeth maintained an unabashed interest in the sensational and the racy:

She thinks Fatty Arbuckle in the present murder case against him should be found guilty. . . . She's dying to read "The Sheik". . . . She has recited all her risque jokes for me, and brought out the latest copy of the Wampus Cat, dirty little rag published at Leesville, Louisiana.

Facing page
Top
The faculty of Pollard High School is pictured in the 1920s. Mrs. E.B. Grogan, at top, became the first woman principal in Beaumont. Courtesy, Tyrrell Historical Library.

Bottom
The Beaumont Exporters of the Texas League brought local residents into the thick of the national sports craze in the 1920s.

They became a Detroit Tigers farm team in 1930 and such well-known stars as Hank Greenberg, Rudy York, Carl Hubbell, and "Schoolboy" Rowe played for them. Courtesy, Business Men's Studio.

Above
Florence Stratton, shown here in 1900, wrote for the Beaumont Enterprise in the 1920s, providing a column of light gossip and local history called "Susie Spindletop's Weekly Letter." While with the paper, she started the "Milk and Ice" and the "Empty Stocking" funds which are still carried on by the Beaumont Enterprise Company. Her history of Beaumont was published in 1927. Courtesy, Tyrrell Historical Library.

Browne, while shocked at much of Elizabeth's behavior, liked her and reluctantly admired her self-confidence, her *savoir faire*, and beneath the gorgeous red curls, her intelligent, inquiring mind. This ambivalence was doubtless shared by many others as the new attitudes of the Roaring Twenties continued to intrude on a conservative and traditional way of life.

The furor over declining morals had no effect on local prosperity, for the city continued to grow. As 1929 dawned, Beaumonters had no reason to doubt that their city would once again reach new economic heights. When the stock market came tumbling down in late 1929, however, it eventually brought with it the rest of the economy, precipitating the downhill slide of the entire nation into the Great Depression.

The Beaumont area did not actually feel the worst effects of the Depression until well into 1931. The rate of the city's growth in the twenties had given the local economy a temporary momentum; the 1931 city directory announced that:

Above
The Frigidaire electric refrigerator made its debut in Beaumont in 1926. Electric refrigeration, however, did not supersede the icebox immediately. Several ice dealers in the city, such as the Crystal Ice Company, continued to do a thriving business in the manufacture and delivery of ice as Beaumont entered the 1930s. Courtesy, Business Men's Studio.

Facing page
Top
Tom W. Shepherd founded the Beaumont Laundry in 1890 on Cypress Street adjacent to the river. The laundry was located on Liberty by the time this picture was taken. Customized Model-T vans and their drivers are poised for collection and delivery. The business, renamed Shepherd Laundry in 1928, remains in the family after three generations. Courtesy, Smythe Shepherd and Business Men's Studio.

Bottom
The Carl Markley Motor Company, Inc., located at Calder and Willow, was ready to sell Fords in spite of the Depression. One advantage to dealers was that by that time there were fewer auto manufacturers in Beaumont than the 40 listed in 1920. By 1934 automobile manufacturing was already settling toward the Big Three (Ford, General Motors, and Chrysler). Courtesy, Business Men's Studio.

The depression that existed throughout 1930 found Beaumont suffering less from unemployment than any city of its class in the Southwest, if not in the entire country.

At last, however, local prosperity was halted; even the thriving petrochemical industry could not save the city from the pernicious effects of a stagnating national economy. Gone were the easy business opportunities of the twenties; established investments failed and no new ones appeared.

Men who had considered themselves more than adequately protected against financial crises were forced to scramble to provide necessities. Some of the fine homes on Calder Avenue went on the market and several well-established downtown stores closed their doors permanently. Only the very wealthiest Beaumonters survived the Depression unscathed.

The low point for Beaumont came in 1933. As if to underscore the grimness of that year, Frank Yount died suddenly November 13. Yount, who had actively aided the

city at least once by donating his personal funds to help meet its payroll, had generally done so much for Beaumont and its citizens that they had come to depend on his leadership and on his company's prosperity. At his death the mayor declared a half day of mourning in his memory. On July 31, 1935, the Yount-Lee Oil Company was sold to Stanolind Oil for $41.6 million, which was divided among its stockholders. The transaction was the largest in the history of the oil industry and the third largest cash transaction in American business to that time. The sale of Yount's company, as well as his death, seemed to take some of the vitality out of Beaumont; after that, the city succumbed to the worst financial period in its history.

In 1929, Beaumonters, with a generous bond issue, had inaugurated an extensive municipal improvement program, which city officials had hoped to complete in the 1930s. However, as the city was unable to find purchasers for the bonds, the program inevitably slowed. Not only special projects were affected; the actual operating budget of the city was jeopardized, as financially strapped citizens became unable to pay ad valorem taxes. Faced with having to run a

city with only a small portion of the necessary funds, officials began drastically to cut back all expenditures. They reduced salaries and dismissed some employees, cut funds to the library and to the schools, and eventually turned off all street lights for several months.

In addition to efforts at financial retrenchment, the city hired attorney Charles Heidrick to collect delinquent taxes. To finance essential expenses, officials authorized a series of "deficiency warrants," in effect IOU's for services rendered, which were redeemable as the city received tax funds.

Both Beaumont and Jefferson County received extensive aid from various government relief programs such as the Public Works Administration, the Works Progress Administration, and the Civilian Conservation Corps, to complete various municipal projects and provide employment. The CCC camp in Beaumont undertook and very nearly completed the mammoth task of building shelters and recreational facilities and improving roads and drainage at Tyrrell Park, a large area donated earlier to the city by Captain W.C. Tyrrell.

Above
The Civilian Conservation Corps, a New Deal agency designed to recruit unemployed youths for environmental improvement work projects, developed Tyrrell Park in the southwest edge of Beaumont. Frank L. Bertschler, head of the Beaumont Parks and Recreation Department, had drawn up a

master plan for this land (donated by Captain W.C. Tyrrell), and CCC members began work on roads, drainage, buildings, and a golf course in November 1935. The program allowed for the cooperation of local businesses and governments. Courtesy, Tyrrell Historical Library.

A number of area families were actually on relief during this time. In 1932 Beaumont received $24,000 in Reconstruction Finance Corporation funds to distribute among Community Chest agencies. The county health officer was given $1,000 a month for relief purposes, and County Judge B.B. Johnson was given shoes and clothing to distribute to the needy.

Even for Beaumonters who were not destitute, life remained a struggle for several years, principally because of the scarcity of cash. Farmers had actually learned to deal with the cash shortage much earlier, for agriculture had been in a slump even during the prosperous twenties. The rice industry had suffered from overproduction in 1909 and prices had remained low ever since. Efforts to raise other money crops such as cotton and figs had met with only moderate success. Consequently, local agricultural agents had encouraged rice farmers to return to subsistence farming—that is, to plant gardens to provide for themselves, then sell any surplus for needed cash. The idea had proved to be so productive that the downtown Nancy Tevis Market, once closed as a poor investment, was reopened in 1929 to provide farmers an outlet for surplus produce.

The rice and oil industries merge in the photo at top of Spindletop field with tank farm in the background. Tractor-drawn binders cut the rice in the fields. Later, the dried bundles were put into the thresher (above), after which the threshed grain was bagged and taken to the warehouse. This threshing crew was on the Rodenbach farm, circa 1925. Courtesy, Texas A & M University Agricultural Research and Extension Center and Business Men's Studio.

Agriculture was so much a tradition in the area that many Beaumonters who were not farmers by profession had, even in better times, maintained small gardens, chickens, and even other livestock in their back yards. During the Depression these agricultural sidelines took on a new importance, not only to provide food, but to furnish a type of currency in a barter system that developed in the absence of cash.

Some things, however, could only be paid for with hard currency. Some Beaumonters, lacking funds to pay their taxes, actually lost their land. Others were able to keep their property but were forced to give up the electricity, the telephone service, or even the natural gas that they had so proudly installed during the previous decade. Many other things, that had once been considered necessities, became luxuries during the Depression and were reluctantly discarded.

As bleak as were the 1930s in Beaumont, even the darkest hours were interspersed with such bright moments as the 1932 Olympics in Los Angeles, which spotlighted Beaumonter Mildred "Babe" Didrikson. As the daughter of Norwegian immigrants, Babe as a young girl had not known the prosperity enjoyed by many in Beaumont during the 1920s. The family of nine lived in a much-added-onto house on Doucette Street in the south end of town. Ole Didrikson, the father, worked as a furniture refinisher, signing on

board tankers when his business was slack; Babe's mother took in washing, while all of the children had odd jobs.

In spite of their hardships, the Didriksons were a close, loving family composed of fiercely competitive natural athletes, of whom Babe was both the most competitive and the most athletic. As she said, "Before I was even into my teens, I knew exactly what I wanted to be when I grew up. My goal was to be the greatest athlete that ever lived."

Her nickname, "Babe," derived from her talent for hitting home runs, was given her by the children with whom she played sandlot baseball. Later, inspired by the 1928 Olympics, she learned to hurdle the seven hedges dividing the yards on her street, persuading one obliging neighbor to trim his hedge to the same height as the rest. Though at the time only slightly over five feet tall, she fought for acceptance on the Beaumont High School basketball team, immediately becoming high scorer when she was finally allowed to play.

Babe's talent was by no means limited to athletics; she was from the beginning determined to be the best at everything she did, whether it was sports, school, or work. At the age of 12, she unloaded empty cans at a fig-packing plant, rolling them down a trough to be filled with figs. In a later job at a gunnysack factory, she so impressed her employer (who originally thought her too small to work) with her speed in sewing sacks together, that he allowed her to leave

Above
Beaumonters sought to augment both local agriculture and real-estate sales by raising figs (left) and citrus fruits. While figs were raised, processed, and marketed extensively, the citrus enterprise failed because temperatures too often dropped below the tolerance level of the trees. Courtesy, Tyrrell Historical Library.

In 1953, at the age of 39, Babe underwent radical surgery for cancer. Bound to play golf again, a year later she won the National Women's Open in Salem, Massachusetts. Despite her hope for recovery, however, her cancer returned and she died September 27, 1956. Babe, a legend long before her death, left a legacy to Beaumonters not only of athletic prowess but of optimism and indomitable courage under adverse circumstances. In order to preserve her legacy for succeeding generations, on November 27, 1976, a grateful and admiring Beaumont dedicated a museum and park to her memory.

By 1939 Beaumont was on the way to economic and social recovery, and survival for most people was no longer the day-to-day struggle it had been. During this year, however, other problems arose; the world situation, long deteriorating, collapsed completely. As hostilities began in Europe, the attention of Beaumonters became riveted overseas in apprehension. The bitter realization came slowly to them, as to the rest of the world, that the Great War had not been, after all, "the war to end all wars." World War II had begun.

whenever she wanted to play ball, realizing she could easily catch up with her work later. In high school she won a prize at the South Texas State Fair with a blue silk dress made in her sewing class; she explained, "... I decided that mine was going to be the most complicated of them all."

In 1930, wearing the blue dress, she traveled by train to Dallas to play basketball for the Employers Casualty Insurance Company team. Each year she played for them, the team advanced to the national finals. Finally, at the 1932 Olympics, she won the javelin throw and the 80-meter hurdle, losing the high jump only because judges ruled she had used improper form; even so, she broke world records in all three events.

Looking for new challenges, Babe then took up golf with her usual determination: "I'd hit balls until my hands were bloody and sore. I'd have tape all over my hands, and blood all over the tape." She won her first important golf tournament in 1935, and for the next 18 years, during which time she met and married wrestler-promoter George Zaharias, she set numerous golf records. Chosen six times as the Woman Athlete of the year, in 1950 she was named Woman Athlete of the Half Century.

Above
The golf course was the site of only one of many triumphs for Mildred "Babe" Didrikson Zaharias. She excelled in every task she undertook and is considered the sports champion of the 20th century. Daughter of Norwegian immigrants, she was raised on Doucette Street in south Beaumont.

Above
Landmarks become especially important in trying times. The O'Brien Oak shaded the 100 feet or more between the O'Brien house and the port to the left. This oak, grown from a sapling brought from Village Creek in 1849, marked the beginning of a path along the riverbank known as Lovers' Lane. Tradition has it that court was sometimes held under its branches. Courtesy, Tyrrell Historical Library.

Chapter VII

Prosperity and Problems

If you don't know where we were, you can't appreciate where we are, and you can't see where we're going.
— *Maurice Meyers, Mayor of Beaumont, in an interview, January 18, 1982*

About lunchtime on Sunday, December 7, 1941, Beaumonters, hearing on their radios the electrifying announcement that the Japanese had attacked Pearl Harbor, realized that they had been plunged into another worldwide conflict. This time the patriotic cheers were tempered with grim knowledge of the struggle that lay ahead; little more than 20 years had passed since the Great War, and memories of its hardships were still undimmed. Nevertheless, citizens threw themselves wholeheartedly into the war effort. The first War Bond drive in town set a national record by being oversubscribed within five hours by $278,000 (for that accomplishment, Beaumont was entitled to have a bomber named after it).

The city's greatest contribution, however, was in industrial output. Many local industries—oil refining, manufacturing of war materiel, shipbuilding—were vital to defense and were mobilized to that purpose. To meet wartime needs, these employers were made to greatly increase their labor forces, luring workers from nearby communities and rural areas with the promise of high wages. Pennsylvania Shipyards, the same firm that, as Beaumont Shipbuilding and Drydock Company, performed a great deal of wartime work in World War I, received more than $100 million in

government contracts to build cargo vessels and naval auxiliary ships. During the war, employment at Pennsylvania shipyards increased from a few hundred to 8,500.

Between 1940 and the middle of 1943, the population of Beaumont jumped from 59,000 to an estimated 80,000; as in the 1901 oil boom, growth quickly outstripped the town's facilities. City buses overflowed; housing shortages became critical. Even Multimax Village, a complex of hastily constructed wooden apartment buildings, could provide for only 600 families; hence, many workers were forced to commute from out of town.

With overcrowding came the more serious problem of racial tension. The numbers of blacks and whites working in close proximity in local industry were much greater than they had ever been; in addition, the great majority of workers were strangers to one another.

Early in the summer of 1943 Beaumont shared the fate of other cities in the nation when racial violence exploded in its streets. The fuse was lit June 4 when a deranged black man beat and raped a young white woman. While attempting to escape he was shot and mortally wounded by police officers. As he lay dying in Martin de Porres, the "Negro ward" at Hotel Dieu, a group of approximately 50

Facing page
The Magnolia, *flagship of the refinery fleet, drew a crowd of onlookers to the Port of Beaumont in 1948. Courtesy, Business Men's Studio.*

Above left
Americans had accused Jack Dempsey of being a slacker during World War I because he did not serve in the armed forces. He came to Beaumont during World War II and fought in a boxing benefit for war bonds on June 22, 1944. Courtesy, Al Vincent.

Above
By 1950 Hotel Dieu Hospital had developed into this complex from the original 19th-century frame building. The black accommodations were in a frame building in the rear. Courtesy, Business Men's Studio.

white men, most of them from the Pennsylvania Shipyards, gathered at the hospital and demanded that the black man be surrendered to them. Police Chief Ross Dickey refused, whereupon the lynch mob dispersed. However, the situation remained tense.

On June 15 a woman living on Eleventh Street told police she had been raped by a black man. By nightfall the story had been circulated and recirculated among the employees at Pennsylvania Shipyards, embellished with each telling. About 9 p.m., 2,000 employees (most of the white workers on that shift) walked off the job and headed toward town. On their way they were joined by others, their numbers swelling to approximately 4,000. First at the police station, then at the courthouse, they demanded that the rapist be given to them for hanging. No suspect was being held at either place, however, and once convinced of this, the mob left, breaking up into small groups. These roving bands headed for the black neighborhoods, both in the downtown area and in the north of town, burning businesses, homes, and automobiles, looting and destroying all property of blacks which lay in their paths, and assaulting blacks wherever they found them.

The entire police force (including the auxiliary) was mobilized. The sheriff's department was also alerted, as were four companies of the 18th battalion of the Texas State Guard, made up of Beaumonters. These law enforcement bodies began to patrol the black neighborhoods, subduing the rioting and arresting a number of people, filling the city and county jails and eventually utilizing the Harvest Club building at the South Texas State Fairgrounds for further detention. However, officials were unable to stop the mobs,

partially because of their inadequate numbers and partially because of their inefficiency; the Texas State Guard troops actually spent much of the night mustering and organizing, first in one place and then another, and in any case were used less for arresting than for patrolling purposes.

Although by dawn the next day the riot, having died for lack of leadership, was for the most part over, within a few hours a total of 2,000 Texas State Guardsmen, Department of Public Safety officers, and Texas Rangers arrived, sent by acting Governor A.M. Aiken. These reinforcements began to patrol black neighborhoods, and, through the use of tear gas, squelched a new uprising of about 200 white shipyard workers at noon that day.

Late in the afternoon of June 16, Aiken declared martial law in the city; troops remained stationed in Beaumont

Above
*A race riot on June 11, 1943,
required the presence of Texas
State Guardsmen, shown
patrolling the streets to prevent
further rioting. Courtesy,
Beaumont Enterprise.*

Above
*Facilities for the storing, milling,
and bagging of rice continued to
grow in Beaumont in mid-century.
Workmen in the Comet Rice Mills
are shown in 1952. Courtesy,
Business Men's Studio.*

for the duration. The city was virtually shut down. City buses ceased operation, and Greyhound buses were instructed to bypass the city. All recreational and public facilities remained closed, as did many businesses. Celebrations for "Juneteenth" (June 19th, the black holiday commemorating the emancipation of slaves in Texas) were cancelled.

By June 20, when it was felt all danger had passed, martial law was lifted; all troops and emergency officers were removed, and Beaumonters resumed their normal activities. They also assessed the riot damage: three men, two black and one white, had died; hundreds of people, mostly blacks, had been injured (among them 52 black draftees waiting at the bus station); and a great deal of property belonging to black citizens had been destroyed. Many had also left town. The white woman who had reported the rape that had triggered the riot was examined by a physician, but no evidence whatever of assault was ever found. Neither was her attacker. The possibility of deliberate sabotage of shipyard production by a foreign power was suspected by authorities, but never substantiated. Of the total of several thousand rioters, only 206 were arrested and brought to the military court, and only 29 of those received penalties of any sort (mostly light fines). Beaumonters seemed less concerned with seeing justice done than they were in putting the unpleasant event behind them. Within a few days production had resumed at Pennsylvania Shipyards, and by July it had returned to normal, although with a much smaller black work force. Area industry remained undisturbed for the remainder of the war.

Bond rallies and industrial output represented only part of Beaumont's contribution to the war effort. Although many Beaumonters served in virtually every area of the military, one particular company, Company C, 143rd Infantry, 36th Infantry Division of the Texas National Guard, was entirely composed of men from the Beaumont area. Before the war was over for them, they had participated in the Africa campaign and had fought bloody battles in the invasions of Italy and Southern France. As the *Beaumont Journal* reported, "Casualties were tragically high."

At last, in 1945, the war ended. Although Beaumont business leaders had been grateful for wartime prosperity, they also were rightly concerned, not only with the prospect of cutbacks in local industrial employment, but also the consequent drop in the number of available jobs at the very moment the young men returning home from war would be most in need of them. Faced with the prospect of dealing with large numbers of unemployed workers, the Chamber of Commerce organized a Postwar Planning Committee to attempt to minimize the impact on the economy.

Because of these efforts and partly because soon after the war Bethlehem Steel Corporation, a thriving, diversified concern, bought out Pennsylvania Shipyards, the adjustment was less traumatic than it might have been. Beaumont's growth, while certainly slow during the immediate postwar era, gradually gained momentum with the advent of several new employers: Goodrich and Firestone synthetic rubber plants, Southern States Steel, Sears, Roebuck and Company, and Baptist Hospital. In addition, a dam was

Above
Until his death in 1948, Hyman Asher Perlstein was one of Beaumont's leaders in business and community services. The year before he died, he received the Exchange Club's Golden Deeds Award for outstanding service to the community. Courtesy, Tyrrell Historical Library.

begun on the upper Neches River, which was to provide not only flood control and irrigation but a valuable recreation area for Southeast Texas.

The years following the war saw an expansion of education, which reached a milestone in 1951 when Beaumont gained a full-fledged four-year college. South Park Junior College, which since its creation in 1923 had experienced exceptional growth, had become Lamar Junior College in 1932, when South Park leaders had felt that its potential service to the community transcended a single school district. In 1940 South Park had united with the other two school districts in the city, Beaumont and French (at that time a separate entity), to form Lamar Union Junior College District. A year later, in 1941, Lamar became an independent state-supported school, although enrollment dropped substantially as a consequence of the war. However, in 1946 returning veterans swelled postwar enrollment to 1,500, creating a sudden demand not only for more teachers and facilities but for an expanded curriculum. In response to this need, the Texas Legislature in 1949 made Lamar a four-year technological college, providing area students with the opportunity to complete their education without ever leaving their hometown.

Beaumonters felt that 1951 was a special year for an additional reason, since it marked the 50th anniversary of the first Spindletop oil discovery. The idea for a special celebration had had its inception in 1941 when Beaumont hosted the Texas Mid-Continent Oil and Gas Association convention. During preparations for this meeting it became clear that the passage of time had blurred the memories of many of the original participants; even the precise location of the Lucas gusher had been forgotten. Ultimately the approximate spot was designated by Scott Myers, a Beaumonter who had grown up in the Spindletop field, and amid much ceremony, a pink granite memorial was unveiled to mark it; but the need had been made apparent for collecting, preserving, and commemorating this vital part of Beaumont's history. Consequently, for the next 10 years, Spindletop Fiftieth Anniversary, Inc., an organization chartered by the State of Texas, carefully laid plans for an elaborate Golden Anniversary year.

The celebration began in January 1951. Particular emphasis had been placed upon honoring the men who had played major roles in the boomtown drama; appropriately, Pattillo Higgins, Al Hamill, and Anthony Fitzgerald Lucas (son of the captain, who had died many years before) were

the principal guests of honor, accompanied by many other veterans of the early oil field days. Beaumont once again became a boomtown, complete with citizens in 1901 attire and a replica of the gusher erected in Sunset Park near the Southern Pacific Depot.

For days programs and exhibits related to Spindletop and the oil industry were presented not only for Beaumonters but for the rest of the nation; the DuPont radio show, "Cavalcade of America," broadcast from Beaumont on January 9 the story of Spindletop. The Melody Maids, a nationally famous singing group led by Beaumonter Eloise Milam, staged on January 5 and 6 a musical production called "Spindletop Review," first presented at City Auditorium and later taken on tour. A gala parade, held on a cold, clear January 10 in downtown Beaumont, included many celebrities, not the least of whom was Alice Carroll Keith, by now an octogenarian and a living legend, driving her antique electric runabout. An elderly Al Hamill proved he was still agile by clambering up the replica of the derrick. Eighty-nine-year-old Pattillo Higgins, in a reprise of his old role, prophesied that the Gulf Coast had gigantic oil reserves as yet untapped. Beaumont briefly regained the national spotlight as townspeople and outsiders alike honored it as the birthplace of the modern oil industry.

Spindletop Hill did not belong exclusively to the past, however; the salt dome was to yield yet another of its riches. Shortly before that anniversary year, Texas Gulf Sulphur had announced plans to build a $12-million plant near the old Spindletop field. The extraction of sulphur, a solid resource, from the earth would cause the land to sink, changing its appearance more than all of the oil drilling had done. Spindletop Hill as a geographic feature would within a few years be gone.

The petrochemical industry continued to expand as more products were made from the petroleum drilled in the area. DuPont constructed a large organic chemical plant on the Sabine-Neches ship channel in the same year that Texas Gulf Sulphur came to Beaumont. By 1954 the petrochemical industry was so important that the *Enterprise* published a "Chemical Empire" issue, which featured not only local oil refineries and chemical plants but the East Texas Pulp and Paper Company (now EasTex, Inc.) at nearby Evadale, which was an outgrowth of the lumber industry.

Improvement of Beaumont's quality of life kept pace with its industrial and economic growth. The town's first

freeway, inaugurating the highway network of the future, was opened in 1955, connecting the Neches River bridge to Eleventh Street. That year a Better Business Bureau was founded, and a United Appeals group was organized.

The postwar era brought new leisure activities for Beaumonters. In 1949 the Neches River Festival, a spring celebration designed to provide a social event for Beaumonters as well as to promote the city to other communities, was held for the first time. Although principally a by-invitation-only affair, some festivities, such as the parade and the boat races, included the general public.

In 1947 KFDM (later KLVI), the area's first radio station, and KRIC (eventually KAYC), begun in the early 1930s, were joined by KTRM and KPBX (later KJET, the area's first black station). KFDM television, Channel 6, a CBS affiliate, began transmitting in 1956, followed a few years later by Channel 4 (NBC) in Port Arthur and Channel 12 (ABC) in Beaumont.

Live entertainment was not forgotten in the development of mass communication. The Little Theater (now the Beaumont Community Players) and the Beaumont Music Commission, founded in the 1920s, were joined in 1953 by a semiprofessional Beaumont Symphony Orchestra, and 10 years later by the Beaumont Civic Opera.

In 1957 the city administration annexed 40.1 square miles of surrounding area. By the acquisition of Rosedale, Voth, and Amelia, unincorporated communities to the north and west of town, the population increased from 104,416 to 122,800. Thus Beaumont, bounded on the east by the Neches River, was, after the annexation, bounded on the north by one of its tributaries, Pine Island Bayou.

Such expansion created the opportunity in Beaumont for an economic innovation: the suburban shopping center. Two opened in 1957; Beaumont Village served residents in the recently added north section of town, while Gateway Shopping City accommodated shoppers in the city's new

Top
Pattillo Higgins (second from left) and Al Hamill (second from right) returned in 1951 to celebrate the golden anniversary of the Lucas Gusher. Scott Myers (left) and Marion E. Brock (right) were charter members of the Lucas Gusher Monument Association. Courtesy, Business Men's Studio.

Above
Price Daniel, Governor of the State of Texas, was Parade Marshal for the 12th annual Neches River Festival in 1960. Courtesy, Business Men's Studio.

Above
Mobil, formerly Magnolia, is Beaumont's largest and oldest refinery. The late Lloyd Baker captured its mechanical complexity with his camera in 1945. Courtesy, Business Men's Studio.

west end. These facilities proved to be a mixed blessing; while they distributed goods to outlying areas, they contributed to the eventual deterioration of the city's central business district.

In 1954, in the wake of the landmark Supreme Court decision, *Brown* v. *Board of Education of Topeka*, which held that the doctrine of "separate but equal" facilities was unconstitutional, Beaumont was faced with the necessity of drastically altering its social structure. The rigid segregation, which since Reconstruction had governed the lives of Beaumonters, suddenly had no legal reason for existence. In Beaumont, as well as in most of the South, people apprehensively awaited the unknown.

It fell to the local chapter of the National Association for the Advancement of Colored People to test the case in a Beaumont court. The NAACP, after its reorganization in 1930, had gradually grown through its ties with the Barnwell Community Center, a religious and social gathering place for blacks, and the Negro Goodwill Council, a group which brought attention to inequities in the local school districts. The NAACP, however, had never attracted a large following from the black community.

In spite of small numbers and avowedly peaceful intentions, the NAACP was still regarded by most white Beaumonters in the 1950s as a dangerously radical group. In an attempt to overcome this image, several blacks launched a

Above
*The Jefferson Amusement
Company opened the Gaylynn
Theater on Eleventh Street in 1949.
The Beaumont Civic Band, led by
Tony Palumbo, gave a concert
which was followed by a cartoon
and the feature,* The Girl from
Jones Beach, *starring Ronald
Reagan and Virginia Mayo.
Courtesy, Business Men's Studio.*

campaign to promote better race relations while still advocating black equality. Foremost among these leaders was Dr. Ed D. Sprott, Jr.

Ed Sprott, long active in affairs of the black community, was a member of a remarkable local family. His parents, Ed and Myrtle Sprott, who had each moved to Beaumont about the turn of the century, were married there in 1906, buying a home on Roberts Avenue. There they reared five sons and four daughters. Each child, knowing it was expected of him or her to attend college, worked to help pay tuition and board (since blacks were unable to attend Lamar, they had to go away to school), the older ones aiding the younger ones. All nine did indeed receive college degrees, with three eventually earning M.D.'s, one a Ph.D., and one an M.A.

Sprott, a member of the NAACP when integration became an issue in Beaumont, believed mutual cooperation to be preferable to legal action, and joined the Beaumont United Racial Council in the hope of working out a gradual process of integration. After expending considerable time and effort with no apparent progress, Sprott reluctantly concluded that integration would require court action. His comments on this decision were quoted by *Enterprise* Editor Robert W. Akers:

We will continue to pay our taxes and serve our community and defend our country in any emergency; yet, at the same time, we shall forever work for a speedy realization of our full civil liberties.

Sprott ended his statement with a challenge to Beaumonters to make integration work:

It is my profound belief that there is as much latent good in Beaumont as there is anywhere in the world. The contemporary problem for men of good will is to see that this latent good is harnessed for constructive, creative, democratic social change. If this is done, the demagogues who would seek to exploit the primitive passions of the people will be left lonely and afraid.

On June 23, 1955, four members of the NAACP, represented by attorneys Theodore Johns and Elmo Willard, brought suit against city officials to desegregate two parks in the city, Central and Tyrrell. (These were chosen as least controversial, as they were less crowded than others and

had no swimming pools.) On September 7, 1955, Judge Lamar Cecil of the Fifth Circuit Court stated that all blacks had "free and unrestricted use and enjoyment of Central and Tyrrell Parks. . . .''

Willard and Johns subsequently filed suit in U.S. District Court March 14, 1956, to desegregate Lamar College. Two blacks had applied for admission and had been refused on the grounds that the state legislature had designated Lamar a white school; the NAACP wished to have the restriction declared unconstitutional. Judge Cecil's decision was consistent with his earlier one; he ruled that Lamar would integrate the following fall.

Twenty-six blacks registered for the fall session at Lamar in 1956; however, some citizens chose to protest the decision. On October 2, the first day of class, black Lamar students were met by white pickets. For the next three days there was general harassment of faculty and of students, both black and white, by picketers. Eventually both teachers and students complained to Lamar President F.L. McDonald; he in turn complained to Mayor Jimmie Cokinos, who ordered the picketers to leave. Three were arrested, and order was ultimately restored.

Within the boundaries of the campus, classes had been held from the first day without incident. Integration at Lamar, after this initial confrontation, proceeded peacefully if perhaps too slowly for some. The athletic program was integrated in spring 1962 with the signing of Anthony Guillory by football coach J.B. Higgins (even though many segregated colleges thereafter struck Lamar from their football schedules), and by fall 1963 all facilities, including dormitories, dining halls, and the student union, were offi-

Above
The E.D. Sprott family, pictured in 1951, represents a remarkable commitment to education and professional achievement. The elder Sprott supported the education of his sons and daughters from his earnings as a postal worker. Standing from left to right are Curtis B. Sprott, M.D.,

Oliver W. Sprott, B.A., Lorraine Whittier, B.A., Myrtle Deplanter, B.A., Waurine Anthony, B.A., Maxie Sprott, M.D., and James T. Sprott, Ph.D.; seated, Mildred White, M.A., Edward Daniel Sprott, father, Myrtle Mills Sprott, mother, and E.D. Sprott, Jr., M.D. Courtesy, Myrtle Sprott Deplanter.

cially open to blacks.

In May 1960 a series of sit-ins were held in Beaumont for the purpose of bringing attention to segregation in public facilities. A group of black Lamar students, who were also members of the local youth NAACP chapter, entered the dining areas of stores in the downtown area and Gateway. The lunchrooms immediately closed. Although the sit-

ins had no direct result, they accomplished their purpose; as one of the participants stated, "We are trying to arouse the South to know just how we feel about the places with which we deal."

Perhaps the most traumatic and certainly the most lengthy phase of integration in Beaumont was that of

the two public school districts. This process began in 1962, when NAACP attorneys Johns and Willard filed suit to integrate the Beaumont Independent School District (which by then included French District schools). The district subsequently adopted a plan to integrate one grade per year, beginning in September 1963 with the first grade, until all grades were integrated, but this ruling was later overturned. In December 1964 the Beaumont District integrated all 12 grades simultaneously, giving students "freedom of choice" to attend any school within the district.

South Park began its integration program in 1965 by establishing freedom of choice. However, this was to prove unsatisfactory, as was the Beaumont plan. Both districts were soon to be ordered by the Federal Court to further alter their plans to achieve racial balance.

In early 1961 Beaumont, along with the rest of Jefferson County, received a great deal of unwelcome publicity in the form of a visit by the General Investigating Committee of the Texas House of Representatives. Beaumont had been an "open city" for many years; that is, illegal elements had been allowed to operate so long as they remained in their designated area. By the 1930s the "red light" district (within the area enclosed by Crockett, Jefferson, Bonham, and Trinity streets) was a well-established hotbed of drinking, gambling and prostitution.

During World War II most of these illicit establishments had been closed by a patriotic city administration to pacify administrators at nearby army bases, who had declared the areas off limits to military personnel. After 1945, however, hotels and bars reopened; this time, many were outside the "Deep" Crockett Street area, and no substantial effort was made to stop them. So accepted was their presence that a new generation grew up accustomed to punchboards in public eating places, bookies who worked high-school campuses, clubs where minors could easily buy liquor, and brothels, operating as openly as ordinary hotels.

In 1960 the problem of vice in the county had come to the attention of a state House investigating committee chaired by Representative Tom James of Dallas. Apparently fearing the takeover of local crime by national organizations, the committee was in the process of exposing and eradicating pockets of vice all over the state. As the *Enterprise* editor said, the probe "staved off a plan by national gambling interests to open up Texas this year."

Officers of the Texas Department of Public Safety were sent to gather evidence; then on December 3, 1960, Texas

Above
Lamar University, under a 1956 court order, was among the first southern colleges to be integrated. Pickets at the entrance to the campus harassed black students for several days before city officials responded to requests for law enforcement from President F.L. McDonald and the student body. Courtesy, Beaumont Enterprise.

Facing page
Top left
John W. Leonard, his sister Hannah, and her husband T.A. Lamb were among those who founded St. Mark's Episcopal Church in 1877. The building was completed in 1942 at Calder and Pearl. Courtesy, Business Men's Studio.

Top right
Charles Charlton, Usan Hebert, Luther Shotwell, and Mary Ann Blanchette participated in the founding of the Live Oak

Missionary Baptist Church (black) in 1868. The congregation worshiped in this building on Neches Street until 1966. Courtesy, Lewis W. Johnson.

Middle
First Christian Church was built at Magnolia and North in 1905. Courtesy, Business Men's Studio.

Bottom left
Members of the St. James United Methodist Church (black) worshiped in this building on Neches and College streets until

1961, when they moved to a location on Blanchette Street. Courtesy, Myrtle Sprott Deplanter.

Bottom right
Mrs. Jeff Chaison and her sister brought Presbyterianism to Beaumont, helping to organize the First Presbyterian Church in 1880. The church moved to this building in 1911. In 1921 First and Central Presbyterian churches merged to form Westminster Presbyterian Church. Photo by Wesley Norton.

Rangers conducted a series of raids in Beaumont, Port Arthur, and other parts of Jefferson County. Armed with this evidence, the five-man investigating committee (called locally the "James Committee") convened a hearing January 4, 1961, in the Federal Building in Beaumont, to bring to public view the status of crime in the area.

During the three days of the hearings, which were televised live over Channel 6 to an understandably enormous local audience, more illegal activity was exposed than many Beaumonters had believed existed—and certainly more than any had wished to acknowledge. Allen Wegemer, a former *Beaumont Journal* reporter who in 1955 had written a series of articles on vice in Jefferson County, testified that in researching his subject he had seen widespread gambling, violation of liquor laws, and prostitution in area clubs and saloons. More disturbingly, he also testified that he was treated with indifference or hostility by local law enforcement officials. After Wegemer had brought gambling charges against a local operator, a grand jury no-billed the gambler; subsequently, the reporter was warned by an assistant district attorney of possible danger to himself if he persisted in his investigations.

Witnesses were either only too willing to testify or inexplicably silent, invoking the Fifth Amendment when questioned. Those who spoke, and they were numerous, provided all that the committee needed to hear about bookmaking, gaming, slot machines, liquor sales to minors, teenage prostitutes, and plain brown envelopes of money left on desks and on back seats of cars. With each testimony the picture grew darker.

After the hearing the committee published its scathing final report: "Committee personnel found flourishing in Jefferson County the oldest, largest, and best-organized vice operation in Texas. Operating openly, brazenly, and with immunity from law enforcement were gambling, bookmaking, prostitution, liquor law violations and narcotics traffic."

The committee graphically and prophetically described a city given over to criminal elements:

Apathy. Bribery. Corruption. These are the ABC's of lawlessness. Decay is the next stage in the alphabetical progression. . . . It is accepted that in any community where vice flourishes and the citizens don't seem to care, the town begins to decay. . . . Tax rates increase. Young people leave the city. Unemployment becomes chronic. Vacancies appear in buildings. Traffic jams occur. The town begins a slow death.

The committee concluded ominously: "These are general symptoms. Many are obvious in Jefferson County."

Beaumonters, at last roused or shamed into making a conscientious effort to end what had undoubtedly been an undesirable and dangerous symbiosis of crime and local law, set out to eradicate what they could no longer ignore. Within a few days, the chief of police had been replaced with the assistant chief; there was a rash of firings and resignations among the remaining members of the police department as well as in city and county offices. A group of citizens organized the United Citizens for Law Enforcement to serve as a watchdog over local government. The grand jury session for the first quarter of 1961, with Samuel Landrum as foreman, returned innumerable charges against individuals for gambling, liquor violations, and prostitution. Eventually removal suits were filed on the Jefferson County sheriff and the district attorney.

The work of the James Committee brought to public attention a well-known but rarely seen Beaumonter: Rita Ainsworth, popularly known as "Miss Rita," the proprietress of the Dixie Hotel on Crockett Street. Born in Oregon of well-to-do parents, Miss Rita was well educated and talented; as a young adult she had toured with various vaudeville shows and at one time had danced with the Ballet Russe de Monte Carlo.

The Great Depression cut short her stage career, however, and during her first marriage she became a prostitute. Fleeing that unhappy marriage, she came to Beaumont, where she found employment in the Crockett Street area, at one of the "cribs" owned by Charles Ainsworth. She later married Ainsworth's son Nathaniel.

After several very hard years, Rita and Nathaniel Ainsworth obtained the Shamrock Hotel on Bowie Street, which they kept until 1946, when Nathaniel died. Rita, with the money Nat left to their two children, bought the Dixie Hotel and began to imbue it with her own distinctive style. Within a short time it became the finest bordello in the area, elegant, smoothly run, and featuring extremely attractive girls. Until the time of the vice probes, the establishment provided Rita a comfortable living. A shrewd businesswoman, she also accumulated quite a bit of real estate in town.

This successful madam had a strong philanthropic

Second Floor of Dixie Hotel   Phone 5-9095

Air Conditioned

DIXIE CLUB

Beaumont, Texas

238½ Crockett St. Between Main & Pearl Sts.

The late Rita Ainsworth (top), Beaumont's leading madam, was a prosperous businesswoman until after the vice probe in 1961. She has been described as having extraordinary grace and dignity. Shown here are her business card and the Dixie Hotel, her place of business. Courtesy, Mary Lou Ainsworth.

bent, that was seen by very few people. Sometimes as a favor, often on her own initiative, she donated enormous sums of money to various local causes such as churches and Little League baseball teams. Individuals also benefited from her largesse; in one case she actually put a priest through seminary. The third floor of the Dixie Hotel was reserved for several homeless old men who paid a nominal fee of $7 a month to be fed, protected, and cared for by Rita and her servants.

Determined that her daughter's life would be easier than her own had been, Rita spent much of her money to send her to a strict Catholic girls' school in another town. So protective was she that her daughter was in her mid-teens before she became aware of the true function of the Dixie Hotel.

Rita herself had no true protector; she had early learned self-reliance, having often suffered at the hands of unscrupulous, self-serving individuals, particularly her numerous husbands. Yet a part of her was apparently capable of deep sentiment. In an old copy of Rudyard Kipling's *The Seven Seas*, found in her library after her death, is inscribed in her handwriting a verse from Tennyson's *Lady of the Lake*:

> *Such love may be madness.*
> *Was love ever sane?*
> *Such love must be sorrow,*
> *For all love is pain.*

The James Committee investigation ended the days of the Dixie Hotel. A permanent injunction was brought against Rita Ainsworth, and the hotel as a house of prostitution ceased to exist (its name was changed to the "Annex Apartments"). In addition, the Internal Revenue Service ordered her to pay $100,000 in taxes on undeclared income; to comply, she was forced to divest herself of all real-estate holdings except the hotel and her comfortable north end home.

In 1976, in failing health and in need of money, she sold the Annex Apartment building to Gulf States Utilities Company, who then donated it to the Beaumont Heritage Society. Miss Rita Ainsworth died in Houston in 1978 in the care of her daughter, her whereabouts known to practically no one but her name still familiar to Beaumonters who remembered the heyday of the Dixie Hotel.

At some point in the 1960s, it became apparent to many

that Beaumont was no longer keeping pace economically with the rest of the country. Since 1960 postwar growth had slowed to an almost imperceptible crawl. In addition, a community apathy had set in which threatened to sabotage all efforts at recovery. Voters defeated a proposal for urban renewal, which might have infused new life into the city, by a decisive 4 to 1 margin. The booster spirit, which had carried Beaumont through past crises and slumps, seemed strangely absent.

Various factors had contributed to the stagnation. Perhaps the governmental corruption brought out in the 1961 vice probes had created a distrust of elected officials and a consequent reluctance by citizens to cooperate with them. In addition, several city administrations had been characterized by internal dissension, making any sort of progress virtually impossible. During that period one city council member was even recalled in a special election.

To make matters worse, the job market hit a slump. In the early 1960s the petrochemical industry began to automate many of its processes, thus decreasing its work force. In 1970 Sun Oil Company, following its merger with another company, moved from Beaumont, vacating the nine floors it had occupied in the downtown Petroleum Building. Several smaller businesses also closed their doors at this time.

Beaumont began showing alarming symptoms of its economic *malaise.* An ever-increasing number of empty buildings gave the downtown area a deserted air. Young high school and college graduates consistently left the area for jobs in Houston and other cities because Beaumont had nothing to offer, and they had no interest in remaining to improve the situation. The James Committee's description of the eventual fate of a vice-ridden city seemed more and more to fit Beaumont. The 1970 census brought home the unpleasant truth: Beaumont had declined in population, while the overwhelming majority of comparable cities had grown. The city was actually moving backward.

Above
Pipefitters Local No. 195 held its annual picnic at the Southeast Texas State Fairgrounds in 1947. The Pipefitters Union is only one of many unions in the Golden Triangle, the most heavily unionized area in Texas. Courtesy, Business Men's Studio.

An aggressive group of Beaumont business and professional men realized that quick action was necessary. They chose as their primary vehicle the Beaumont Chamber of Commerce, which since its formation in 1903 had filled an essentially ceremonial role, but under its new leadership would play a vital part in Beaumont's development. Elected as Chamber president in 1970, Mark Steinhagen, with other Chamber directors, announced a new emphasis on economic growth, stating emphatically that "superfluous activities, ceremonial functions, and other nonproductive activities of the staff must be discontinued and the Chamber must establish a new image by achieving its goals."

The Chamber formed an Economic Development Committee, with Elvis Mason, a graduate of Lamar and a rising young Beaumont banker, as its chairman. Results were soon evident; the business sector responded with the Economic Development Foundation, Leadership Beaumont (to encourage and develop present and future leadership), and the Central City Development Corporation, a company formed to revive the flagging downtown area.

When Southwestern Bell Telephone Company announced plans to build a $9-million regional office, members of the CCDC, at the instigation of Mason and a young Beaumont lawyer named Robert Keith, contributed $175,000 in additional land costs from their own pockets to persuade Bell to build in the downtown business district, thus achieving a turnaround in the business and professional exodus from the downtown area. Many of the "young Turks," as some termed the group, also began running for local offices, including school board and city council positions, in an effort to provide responsible leadership and to inspire flagging trust in local officialdom.

Beaumonters responded to these efforts with unprecedented cooperation between city government and the private sector. As the town slowly began to move forward once again, its new leaders prepared for the 1970s, a decade which they hoped would bring an era of growth.

Top
This relatively primitive drilling rig was photographed in the Gulf of Mexico in 1957. The search for offshore oil actually began well before the worldwide oil shortages of the 1970s. Courtesy, Business Men's Studio.

Above
Magnolia Drilling Barge No. 4, pictured in 1949, is an example of the offshore drilling equipment built in Beaumont before the 1960s. Courtesy, Business Men's Studio.

Above
Mr. Gus, *built in Bethlehem Shipyards in 1954 for the Shell Oil Company, represents one stage in the rapid evolution of the massive offshore drilling platform. The second Mr. Gus, built in 1957, was the first rig capable of drilling in 180 feet of water. Courtesy, Business Men's Studio.*

Chapter VIII

Today and Tomorrow

Assuredly, there is much to like about Beaumont. Vast leaps in the city's quality of life have been made in the past few years. And although there's still plenty of room for improvement, the new leadership seems aware of the problems and dedicated to solving them. Given such determination, there's no reason to suspect that Beaumont will fail to achieve at least the promise inherent in the episode at Spindletop almost 75 years ago.

—*Article by Keith Elliott*
in Texas Parade, *1975*

At least partially as a result of the imaginative effort of this energetic young faction, Beaumont slowly began to grow again. More importantly, as tangible signs of the new force abroad in the town began one by one to appear, the apathetic, defeatist attitude of Beaumonters imperceptibly began to change for the better. Pride in their city and in their corner of the world began to return, and with it the desire to improve the quality of their lives.

Reflecting this new attitude, Beaumont's citizens in 1971 approved municipal bonds for the first time in almost 50 years, voting $12 million for improvements to the Port of

Beaumont and $18 million for a new library, police station, and water, sewer, and street improvements. These were followed in 1974 by a $28-million bond issue covering construction of a new civic center, municipal office building, riverfront park, and covered arena at the South Texas State Fairgrounds.

Municipal improvements were not enough, however. New businesses were needed to provide fresh job opportunities for prospective citizens. Capital from these new ventures, plus additional money brought into town by visitors and convention delegates, was essential to boost the area's cash flow. Beaumont's greatest task was first to attract attention to the area, and, that accomplished, to ensure that people received a favorable impression of the city.

In the early 1970s the Beaumont Chamber of Commerce launched an extensive advertising campaign, its purpose to attract new business to Beaumont. Under the Chamber's auspices, a Visitor Information Center was built in 1974 on Interstate Highway 10 at Walden Road to welcome incoming travelers and to furnish them with information about Beaumont, while a Convention Bureau set up a tour of points of interest in the city.

As a result of the Chamber's campaign, outside capital did indeed begin to notice Beaumont and to like what it saw. Metro Airlines began commuter flights from Jefferson County Airport to Houston Intercontinental in 1972. Georgetown Steel Company announced in 1973 the construction of a $100-million rolling mill on the east side of the Neches River directly across from Beaumont. Other new firms followed Georgetown's example. In addition, several already established businesses, including Malone and Hyde Foods and First Federal Savings and Loan Association, constructed new facilities, some in the downtown sector. By 1976 new or expanded businesses in Beaumont were providing between 400 and 500 additional jobs. That same year Beaumont hosted 74 conventions, with at least 33,000 delegates in attendance, bringing several million dollars into the community.

During this recovery period, one of the most successful economic projects, both from the standpoint of profit for the developers and the enormous amount of capital brought into town, was the construction of an enclosed shopping center to serve not just one area, but all of Southeast Texas and Southwest Louisiana. Parkdale Mall, completed in 1973 in Northwest Beaumont, was the inspiration of Ben Rogers, a local investor and real-estate developer.

Facing page
Lamar University had expanded to this size by 1976. The John and Mary Gray Library, Lamar's first multistory building, awaited application of exterior brick for completion. Courtesy, Business Men's Studio.

Above
The 13-story Petroleum Building, completed in 1961, was the first major business building to go up in downtown Beaumont since 1928. It was part of the American Center, which also included the separately owned, five-story American National Bank building. The two shared the same design and a connecting terrace with trees, fountains, and walkways. Courtesy, Business Men's Studio.

Ben Rogers and his brothers Sol, Vic, and Nate, came originally from Chicago to Beaumont in the latter part of the 1930s. In Beaumont they began a family business, Texas State Optical Company (which became one of the largest optical concerns in the country). However, through the vision and energy of Ben, they soon began to diversify their interests. One of their first major projects was Gateway Shopping City, which, despite pessimistic predictions by economic forecasters, prospered from its beginning, soon influencing other firms to move nearby to share the wealth. Parkdale Mall, which opened 16 years later, was over twice as big as Gateway, with 55 stores (almost a million square feet) in a completely enclosed shopping space. The Mall, like Gateway, became the focal point for an extensive retail area.

Ben Rogers' philanthropies increased proportionately to his success. Countless individuals and organizations were the grateful recipients of his generosity. Largely through his direction, the Babe Zaharias Memorial Museum was completed and dedicated in 1976. Rogers was also the force behind the creation of Orleans Plaza, a strip in downtown Beaumont which was outfitted with trees, benches, and old-fashioned streetlights. Orleans Plaza beautified the street in front of the Rogers brothers' offices in the San Jacinto Building, at the same time revitalizing a four-block shopping area downtown. The accomplishments of Ben Rogers and his brothers, whether for private profits or for the public weal, always ended by benefiting Beaumont.

The economy in Beaumont had progressed so far by 1975 that a nationwide recession that year had very little effect on the area. Momentum, and a sound economic base, carried the city through the slump without faltering. In 1978 Beaumont was named by *Money* magazine as the town with the most potential for future growth in the entire country.

One of the most ambitious and farsighted projects undertaken in the push to save Beaumont was the creation of the Planning Economic Progress committee (PEP). Over the years union members and employers in the Beaumont area had come to view any construction site as a potential battleground. Strikes and walkouts were so commonplace that they were written into the cost of any construction project. Consequently, building was more expensive in Beaumont than in other communities; in addition, schedules were unpredictable.

Soon after election in 1979 to his first term as mayor, Maurice Meyers addressed himself to this problem, for he realized it was one of the greatest impediments to new development in Beaumont. All of the city's resources and facilities were to no avail if, as he said, the area was not "cost-competitive." Mayor Meyers called a meeting on September 5, 1979, of 38 local leaders, representing both labor and management. Together they pledged to improve area labor-management relations by preventing strikes through negotiation and communication rather than waiting to set-

Above
The Rogers brothers (left to right), Sol, Ben (seated), Vic, and Nate, arrived in Beaumont in the middle of the Depression and went into business as optometrists. The Texas State Optical Company, specializing in providing affordable glasses for the public, eventually expanded to 109 outlets. In 1955 the brothers formed Rogers Brothers Investments, and have since been prime movers in Beaumont business, community development, and charitable endeavors. Courtesy, Ben Rogers.

Above
In 1946 the late A.W. Schlesinger (second from left) began providing facilities for the elderly in a run-down building on Ashley Street. This groundbreaking was for the construction of one of the largest and most modern geriatric facilities in Texas, which opened its first unit in 1970. Left to right are H.E. Dishman, Schlesinger, Congressman Jack Brooks, Roy Nelson, and John Green. Courtesy, Business Men's Studio.

tle them after picket lines went up. Thus PEP was born. As its report stated:

PEP is not a substitute for collective bargaining but rather a formula for dealing with problems that lie beyond the scope of contracts and corporate management. Its tools are teamwork and the pooling of ideas rather than tradeouts and bargaining. Its goals are not limited gains from hard-won concessions, but big results and shared benefits from effective, cooperative planning and implementation.

In the two years after its creation, PEP was involved in settling over 200 disputes, of which about 85 percent were settled before they became walkouts. One of the town's thorniest problems no longer automatically presented an obstacle to economic growth.

Also treating the subject of industrial productivity was the John E. Gray Institute, created in 1981. The brainchild of former Beaumonter Elvis Mason (since the early 1970s a resident of Dallas), the Institute, located on the Lamar University campus, was for the specific purpose of studying the petrochemical industry along the labor-intensive Gulf Coast. This project, however, was of much greater magnitude than the PEP, for the Gray Institute's work was to be of national scope. Directors and staff members were men and women of national standing in their respective fields.

The idea was so well received that over 90 percent of the operating budget for the first five years of the Institute was raised by the time of the groundbreaking ceremonies. The Gray Institute, while performing an invaluable function regarding labor-management problems, would also bring prestige to Beaumont and to Lamar University.

The name of the Institute appropriately honored a man who had for many years been a leader in area business and education. Associated with Lamar since its creation in 1923, first as a student, then as a teacher, John Gray became president in 1942, serving until 1952, when he joined the business community for the next 20 years as an executive officer of First Security National Bank in Beaumont. Gray returned to Lamar as president in 1972, remaining until 1976, when he retired to further serve the University in advisory roles. He had also become a power in statewide and national educational circles, having served as the first chairman of the Coordinating Board of the Texas College and University System and as a member of the Executive Committee of the Education Commission of the States. Throughout his lengthy career, Dr. Gray had remained an abiding supporter both of Lamar and of Beaumont. When ground was broken on January 21, 1982, for the John Gray Institute building, the *Enterprise* stated, "The Gray Institute promises to be a significant and worthy asset to Lamar, Beaumont and the entire region—just like, in fact, the man for whom it is named."

The John Gray Institute's location on its campus came at the end of an especially momentous decade for Lamar. It had grown as a four-year college, both physically and

academically; in 1971 the college was designated a university with the expectation that it would thus be able to increase its services to the community. After 1972, under John Gray's leadership, the college greatly increased the size of its campus and undertook an extensive building program. In 1973 Lamar University celebrated its 50th anniversary, commemorating the occasion by issuing a medallion on which was embossed the likeness of the Texas statesman for whom the college was named, Mirabeau Bonaparte Lamar.

Public education in Beaumont had, in the 1970s, expended much of its energy in a continuation of the strenuous integration process. The United States Justice Department, unhappy with the progress of integration in both school districts, brought suits to force them to comply with federal guidelines. The Beaumont District in 1976 was ordered by United States District Judge Joe J. Fisher to

In spite of delays, frustrations, and many hard feelings, most citizens remained hopeful for the eventual stabilization of the school situation. Perhaps an article in the *Enterprise* best expressed their feelings:

In all fairness, historians could never align Beaumont's racial strife with that of Selma, Alabama, or Wilmington, Delaware, which is why many Beaumonters, black and white, say they weathered the civil rights movement of the 1960s to live and send their children to schools here.

In their newfound community consciousness, Beaumonters were able to point with pride to a valuable local resource, one which for years had been an important export: talent. A number of people born or reared in Beaumont and

replace its "freedom of choice" plan of integration with a more satisfactory one. As a result of the order, the black high school, Charlton-Pollard, was combined with one of the white schools to form Beaumont-Charlton-Pollard High School, its home the former Beaumont High School campus. Boundaries were extensively redrawn to achieve a satisfactory racial mix.

South Park had originally replaced its freedom of choice policy with a detailed integration plan in 1970 which, because of "white flight," was challenged in 1976 by the Justice Department. After a five-year hiatus, the case was finally decided in August 1981 by Judge Robert M. Parker, who ordered desegregation for the entire school district in September of 1981, to be accomplished by random selection of students.

its environs had gone on to represent the city well in music. Beaumonter Harry James became famous in the era of the big bands in the 1940s, not only as a trumpet player but as a bandleader. In the 1950s disc jockey and entertainer J.P. Richardson, known as the "Big Bopper," gained national acclaim with his record, "Chantilly Lace," not long before he was killed in a plane crash. During the "hard rock" years of the 1960s, Johnny and Edgar Winter, brothers from Beaumont, traveled to New York, where they performed with separate groups; their diverse musical skills were well received, not only by audiences but also by other artists. Port Arthur native Janis Joplin, who died in 1970, became a cult figure, drawing enormous crowds with her style of singing, often reminiscent of performers from the Southeast Texas-Southwest Louisiana region.

Above
*Following the westward expansion of the city, the South Park School District built Forest Park High School, now Vincent Junior High, in the Amelia area in 1961.
Courtesy, Business Men's Studio.*

Country music in the area has its roots in Acadian (Cajun) Louisiana as well as the Old West. Aubrey "Moon" Mullican, a country singer from Beaumont, scored a hit in the 1940s with his recording of "Jolie Blon'," a popular Cajun song. The era of the "singing cowboys," in the 1940s and early 1950s, brought lasting fame to Nederland's Tex Ritter, best known for his recording of the song from the movie *High Noon.* Country star Billie Jo Spears, while still a teenager in Beaumont, began singing at Neva's, a night club in the Beaumont suburb of Voth. George Jones, hailing from Vidor, just east of Beaumont, was in 1976 named Country Singer of the Year. One of his first hits was "White Lightnin'," written by the "Big Bopper," J.P. Richardson.

In the field of visual arts, Beaumont produced Herring Coe, artist and sculptor of national reputation, who crafted among other works the statue of Dick Dowling at the Sabine Pass battleground. Sculptor David Cargill of Beaumont became well known in the area for works displayed on the grounds of the Wilson Art Museum as well as the statue of Mirabeau B. Lamar on the Lamar University campus. Bucky Milam, son of Melody Maids' mentor Eloise Milam and grandson of Dr. Lena Milam, a longtime Beaumont music educator, achieved prominence in New York, not only as a painter but as a jazz trumpet player.

The area has been perhaps even more productive of sports figures. In football, in particular, Beaumont has been so outstanding that the National Football League in 1973 named it the Pro Football Capital of the world. Perhaps this abundance of skill was due in part to a local phenomenon known as the "Soul Bowl." This annual game, played in the days before integration, brought together the coaches of the city's two black high schools: Clifton Ozen of Hebert and Willie Ray Smith of Charlton-Pollard. So strong was the rivalry and so heated the yearly conflicts that the game was always a sellout. The resulting interest in and support for football at both schools induced athletic youngsters to play. Hebert supplied a great many players to the professional ranks, among them Anthony Guillory (Lamar's first black athlete), brothers Miller and Mel Farr, and Jerry Levias. At Charlton-Pollard, two of Coach Smith's three sons, Bubba and Tody, played professional football. From French High came Louis Kelcher and Gus Holloman. O.A. "Bum" Phillips, born in Orange, 25 miles east of Beaumont, played football at Lamar Junior College and coached at Nederland and Port Neches-Groves high schools before eventually becoming head coach, first of the Houston Oilers, then the New Orleans Saints.

Mrs. Fayetta Donovan (right), retired nurse and avid fisherwoman, is the granddaughter of Woodson Pipkin, pioneer educator and churchman. Her son Clarence A. Jackson (above right), shown in uniform during the Korean War, is Director of Special Programs for the Beaumont Independent School District. His daughter Stephanie Ann Jackson (above) is an accountant with a Houston firm. She was Miss Black Lamar in 1979. Courtesy, Wesley Norton (Donovan photo) and Fayetta Donovan (Jackson photos).

Area Golden Gloves tournaments promoted interest in boxing; at least two local champions became well-known professional boxers. Paul Jorgensen from Port Arthur was a contender in the 1950s for the World Lightweight Championship, while Olympic boxer James "Bubba" Busceme aspired to the lightweight title in the 1980s.

Marty Fleckman of Port Arthur and Bert Weaver and Bruce Lietzke of Beaumont all went on to become professional golfers after developing their skills on local courses. Professional female golfers from Beaumont, in addition to Babe Zaharias, include Susie McAllister and Lamar alumnus Clifford Ann Creed.

The cultural atmosphere of a town is perhaps the surest indicator of the quality of life within it. During the decade of the 1970s, culture in Beaumont began to come into its own. In addition to the Beaumont Symphony and the Beaumont Civic Opera, which continued to bring classics to city eyes and ears, many new cultural groups were either established or expanded. The Beaumont Art Museum, which had grown phenomenally since its modest beginning in 1950 and its sojourn after 1970 in the J. Cooke Wilson home, announced in 1981 the acquisition of the site of the old Jefferson County Tuberculosis Hospital on Delaware Street, and the building of a new museum building. A Beaumont chapter of Young Audiences, Inc., was established in the spring of 1973 through the Junior League of Beaumont. Programs such as Young Audiences, by utilizing professional performers on the faculty of Lamar University, fostered cooperation between the community and the university, to the immeasurable benefit of both institutions.

In the decade of the 1970s, the arts groups in Beaumont came under the patronage of their own particular good angel, Carol Tyrrell (Mrs. Wesley W.) Kyle. Mrs. Kyle, associated with two pioneer Beaumont families both by blood and by marriage, was to prove the most generous sponsor of the arts in the history of the town, often underwriting the entire cost of a concert or performance singlehandedly. All the citizens of Beaumont, present and future, owe Mrs. Kyle a lasting debt of gratitude for permanently influencing the growth of the arts in the city.

As Beaumonters began to view their present achievements with pride and confidently to voice their hopes for the future, they also began to develop a consciousness of their town's past and to realize that its heritage, unique to itself, was well worth preserving. In 1967 a group of history-conscious citizens formed the Beaumont Heritage Society, an organization dedicated to preserving the city's past, and announced as their first project the restoration of the still-extant John Jay French home, which throughout its long years of existence had continued to be used as a private residence. The Junior League of Beaumont purchased the house from its current occupants, Mr. and Mrs. M.A. Merchant, then donated it to the newly formed Heritage Society. Over a period of time the Society restored it to its 1845 appearance, reconstructing many of the original features of the house, including a wash house, corn crib, smoke house, and tannery. Opened in 1970, the John Jay French Museum, as it is now known, is the center for Beaumont's "remembrance of things past," featuring many programs on various aspects of life in mid-19th-century Beaumont, including a candlelight Christmas tour, when the house is decorated as it might have been in 1845.

Above
Carol Tyrrell Kyle, granddaughter of Captain W.C. Tyrrell, has long been Beaumont's most generous patron of the arts. In addition to giving large cash donations in behalf of all the arts, she has underwritten the appearance of many well-known performing artists year after year. She received the Golden Deeds Award from the Exchange Club in 1978. Courtesy, Tyrrell Public Library.

Facing page
Among the local buildings listed in the National Register of Historic Places is the Kyle building. Built by Wesley W. Kyle in 1931 in the 300 block of Orleans Street, it is one of the finest examples of Art Deco in Texas. It is currently being restored for use as an office building by its owners Bruce Reich of Austin and Beaumonters Frederic Seewald and Jack McNeill. Courtesy, Business Men's Studio.

The Heritage Society has also concerned itself with other Beaumont buildings of historic significance. When it was given the Dixie Hotel by Gulf States Utilities Company in 1976, the Society placed deed restrictions upon the building before selling it, thus ensuring its safety. The Society was also instrumental in saving the Sanders house, an 1895 Carpenter Gothic frame dwelling on the river, which it purchased and then resold to Barbara and Alan McNeill in 1981 for their use as an office building. With the help of the city, the Heritage Society commissioned a restoration architect to survey buildings in Beaumont in order to determine which were worth preserving. The resulting SPARE Beaumont Survey, as it was called, has heightened Beaumonters' awareness of the historically significant in their town.

In addition to the activities of the Heritage Society, many individual Beaumonters began undertaking independent restoration projects. The Kyle building, "one of the best examples of art deco architecture in the state," according to one of its purchasers, was bought in October 1981 by Austinite Bruce Reich and Beaumonters Frederic Seewald and Jack McNeill for restoration as an office building. Local designer Bryan Hendrix assumed proprietorship of the Hinchee house, built in 1901 on the corner of Park and Irma streets, with plans to restore it for use as a home and office. Many homes in the old residential neighborhood which included Broadway, Liberty, Laurel, Calder, McFaddin, and North streets were purchased by merchants who, appreciating their aesthetic value, transformed them into stores, craft shops, art galleries, and restaurants. Old Town, as it is called, has become one of Beaumont's most vital, interesting areas.

The Jefferson Theater Preservation Society, formed in the 1970s, made a working facility out of the historic old Jefferson Theater while gradually restoring it to its former grandeur. It now hosts concerts by the Beaumont Symphony and Beaumont Civic Opera, performances by the Beaumont Civic Ballet, visiting artists, and variety shows given by the Beaumont Junior Forum and many other civic organizations.

In honor of Spindletop's 75th anniversary in 1976, a group of citizens raised funds to finance the building of a full-scale replica of Gladys City, near the site of the original boom town. In conjunction with the Spindletop Museum, an institution which houses relics of the early oil industry, the Beaumont Heritage Society yearly conducts a historic folk festival, Spindletop Boom Days, at Gladys City.

The old Romanesque Tyrrell Public Library, formerly the First Baptist Church, which had served until 1974 as Beaumont's main library, assumed yet another role as the

Tyrrell Historical Library, its purpose, while undergoing gradual restoration, to house historical documents and Texana.

Coincidentally, the symbol of downtown Beaumont's future, the new Southwestern Bell Telephone building, was constructed in 1973 practically upon the site of the cabin of Noah Tevis. When workers were excavating for the foundation of the building, they found an ancient cypress-cribbed well. Scrape marks made by old buckets were visible upon its planks, which were still in excellent condition after having been buried for over 150 years. The site of the well, thought to be that of Noah Tevis, is permanently marked with a plaque in front of the building.

In touting their city to other areas, Beaumonters have discovered for themselves that water, the city's premiere resource, has played a major part in its continuing existence. As they did in the early days of Beaumont's history, ships still link the town on the Neches River with the rest of the world. Water also enriches the city's quality of life; the river, the nearby freshwater lakes, and the Gulf provide numerous recreational facilities. Even the heavy rainfall is beneficial; Beaumont is one of the few Sunbelt cities that does not have a water shortage. In the days to come, when oil and gas supplies are exhausted and access to water becomes more and more of a problem, Beaumont's first resource will come full circle, ending by being its most enduring, both for livelihood and for life itself.

Though there have been many drastic changes in this corner of Texas since Henry Millard first stood on Noah Tevis' bluff and planned to build a town, some things will never pass away. From its genesis in Northeast Texas, the Neches River still meanders southward, lazily flowing past Beaumont before emptying its waters into Sabine Lake and then into the Gulf of Mexico. The Big Thicket, much diminished by the depredations of the lumbermen but still an identifiable geographical entity, lies brooding to the northwest of town, but from within the safe boundaries of an 85,000-acre national park. The prairies are now neatly checkered with fields, some planted with rice crops, some dotted with grazing cattle. A little way to the south are the salt marshes near the Gulf, on whose sandy beaches crude petroleum is still deposited by the tides. Far out on the blue-gray waters of the Gulf, the ships, ocean-going tankers and freighters follow the buoys and channel markers that lead them to their destinations, some ending their journeys up the Neches at the Port of Beaumont. The city is still

possessed of every natural advantage that it could ever need.

As the history of Beaumont began with the land, so it must end with the land, which has given generously of its gifts. A community, in developing its own identity, must assume the responsibility of utilizing those natural gifts to its own best advantage, whether that be to grow in size, to improve its inhabitants' way of life, or both. Sometimes with failure, sometimes with great success, the inhabitants of the city of Beaumont have availed themselves of those gifts. It lies with the present generation to explore their full potential, to obtain for themselves and their progeny the highest quality of life, thereby redeeming the implicit pledge made by the land to its people so long ago.

Top
The Southwestern Bell Telephone building, left, was dedicated in 1976 and stands on the approximate site of the Noah Tevis cabin. The foundation allows for 16 additional stories to accommodate expanded service to more than 500,000 phones in the division. Gulf States Utilities is in the process of moving into the new Edison Plaza at the right. Photo by Wesley Norton.

Above
More than 250 ships a year dock at the Port of Beaumont, carrying over 2.5 million tons of goods. Four ships are shown loading food for ports in Japan, Egypt, Ceylon, and Israel. Courtesy, Business Men's Studio.

Chapter IX

Beauty of Past and Present

This scene of the business district, the Port of Beaumont, Mobil Refinery, and the Gulf Coast plain beyond summarizes a great deal of Beaumont's economic history. The island in the harbor has been joined by landfill to the mainland, new docks and storage added, and the Continental Grain exporting facilities built since this photo was taken in the early 1960s. From left to right, the tallest buildings are the old Edson Hotel, the Goodhue Building, the American National Bank Building, the San Jacinto Building (with clock tower), the King Edward Hotel (formerly the La Salle), the courthouse, and the Petroleum Building. Courtesy, Business Men's Studio.

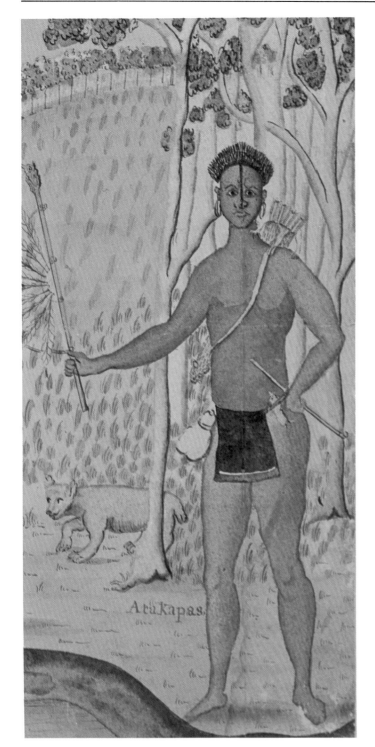

Above
This segment of a painting by Frenchman A. De Batz shows an Attakapas Indian, typical of the early inhabitants of the Southeast Texas area. The Attakapas smeared alligator oil on their bodies to ward off mosquitoes, and were known to engage in cannibalism. They lived comfortably off the land between the Sabine, Neches, and Trinity rivers, moving inland in the winter to hunt and fish. By the 19th century they had virtually disappeared. Courtesy, Peabody Museum, Harvard University.

Top right
The hardwood forest begins to renew itself along a creek bottom in the Big Thicket National Preserve. Photo by Wesley Norton.

Above
Diverse and beautiful plant life populates the Big Thicket National Preserve, which reaches into Beaumont from the north. Often referred to as the "biological crossroads of North America," the Big Thicket includes 84,000 acres in eight land units and four stream corridors. This minimum acreage is designed to preserve the most ecologically significant areas of the original Big Thicket. Pictured here, from among hundreds of rare and beautiful specimens, are the wild bean (left) and Indian pipes. Photos by Wesley Norton.

Facing page
Top
The yards of the Beaumont Ship Building and Dry Dock Company are shown in 1908. Courtesy, Tyrrell Historical Library.

Bottom
Lumberman J. Frank Keith owned this sailing ship, Alice, named for his wife. The Alice carried lumber from Keith's mills but had to be loaded at Sabine Pass since vessels this size could not reach Beaumont before 1908. Courtesy, Jane Clark Owens.

Top left
This painting is based on Frank Trost's famous photograph of the Lucas Gusher. At this stage the gusher was spouting 100,000 barrels of oil a day. Most of the oil was contained in hastily built earthen dikes. Courtesy, Spindletop Museum.

Top right
Spindletop Viewing Her Gusher, *painted by Aaron Arion, was donated by the George W. Carroll family to the Tyrrell Historical Library. Mr. Carroll insisted that the nude figure in the original be clothed, hence the flowing garment. Courtesy, Tyrrell Historical Library.*

Above left
Anthony Lucas, a professional mining engineer born in Austria, shared Pattillo Higgins' vision of striking oil at Spindletop. He eventually realized only $400,000 for himself out of the wealth created by the oil discovery. Courtesy, Spindletop Museum.

Above
Curt Hamill, brother to Al and J.G. Hamill, was in charge of night drilling on the crew that brought in Spindletop. The Hamills were proficient drillers and, with Lucas, significantly advanced drilling techniques. Courtesy, Spindletop Museum.

Facing page
The Spindletop oil field was photographed at night by Lloyd Baker in 1951 as the golden anniversary of Spindletop approached. Courtesy, Business Men's Studio.

Top
Eastern Texas Electric Company, predecessor of Gulf States Utilities Company, operated electric streetcars from 1902 until 1937. Even such a useful service could be the butt of a Beaumont Journal *joke: "One of the beauties of living on the Magnolia car line is that when you miss your car you don't have to wait an hour or so for another. You just walk to the next corner and overtake the one you've missed." Courtesy, Tyrrell Historical Library.*

Above
A postcard in the first decade of the 20th century shows this view of downtown Beaumont. Courtesy, Tyrrell Historical Library.

Facing page
Top
This view is of Pearl Street in downtown Beaumont in the early 20th century. Courtesy, Tyrrell Historical Library.

Bottom
The proprietors of Hotel Beaumont advertised it thus after its opening in the 1920s. Courtesy, Tyrrell Historical Library.

HOTEL BEAUMONT
BEAUMONT, TEXAS

Top
*The Neches Iron Works was but
one of many thriving industries
that developed to service the oil
industry after Spindletop.
Courtesy, Tyrrell Historical
Library.*

Above left and right
*W.C. Averill was a businessman
and developer in the early 20th
century. His residence, unique
among Beaumont homes, appeared
on the face of this postcard circa
1910. Courtesy, Spindletop
Museum (portrait) and Tyrrell
Historical Library.*

Top left
John Henry Phelan came to Beaumont as a salesman in 1903 and founded a wholesale grocery concern in 1913. He became vice president of the Yount-Lee Oil Company and his original $750 investment turned into millions within a few years. Courtesy, Spindletop Museum.

Top right
The John Henry Phelan house was completed in 1929 with wealth from the second Spindletop boom and was lavishly adorned with European furnishing and art. Eventually the Phelans donated the 20-acre block of land as a site for St. Elizabeth Hospital and donated the house as a residence for the Sisters of Charity of the Incarnate Word. Photo by Wesley Norton.

Above
The present McFaddin house on McFaddin Street was built for W.P.H. McFaddin and completed in 1906. Typical of Victorian architecture in its massive and elaborate construction, its five floors (including basement and attic) contain a music room, library, sun parlor, drawing room, dining room, breakfast room, and ballroom (on the third floor). Photo by Wesley Norton.

Top left

St. Anthony's Cathedral at Wall and Jefferson was dedicated on January 27, 1907, thus formally ending the Parish of St. Louis which had been the first Catholic organization in Beaumont. The Cathedral underwent major changes in 1937 when the interior was decorated with oil paintings and stained glass windows depicting the beliefs and symbolism of the Catholic Church. It is considered one of the most beautiful structures of the Roman Catholic Church in the entire

South. Courtesy, St. Anthony's Cathedral.

Top right

Temple Emanuel, with its copper dome and stained glass, was built in 1923. The congregation was first formed under Rabbi Aaron Levy and held services on the second floor of the Central Fire Station until 1900. The first synagogue stood where First Baptist Church now stands. Rabbi Samuel Rosinger, arriving in 1910, served the congregation for more than 50 years. Photo by Wesley Norton.

Above left

This is the fourth building of the First United Methodist Church since its founding at the time of the Civil War. The "spired" church (as distinct from its predecessor, the "domed" church), was completed in 1968 during the pastorate of John Wesley Hardt. Photo by Wesley Norton. Courtesy, First United Methodist Church.

Above

Members of the First Baptist Church have built four times in downtown Beaumont since their founding in 1872. The sanctuary in the foreground opened for worship in 1925, with the educational wings added as the church grew. With more than 7,000 members, First Baptist Church is one of the largest Southern Baptist Churches in the nation. Courtesy, Business Men's Studio and First Baptist Church.

Beaumont's "Old Town" is a collection of more than 40 unusual shops and restaurants in an older neighborhood between downtown and Eleventh Street. The Apple Box on Calder (top left) sells antiques and gifts, the Old Town Pub on Broadway (top right) serves sandwiches, salads, and fancy frozen drinks, and the Black-Eyed Pea (middle right), located in the old Sim Parrish house on Broadway and Seventh, specializes in home-style southern cooking. Photos by Wesley Norton.

Middle left
The old and new converge where the Edison Plaza of Gulf States Utilities dominates the skyline. To the left is the old Edson Hotel which housed the general offices of Gulf States Utilities prior to their occupancy of the new building at center. At right is the Goodhue Building, one of the splendid buildings of the 1920s still in use. Photo by Wesley Norton.

Above left
This view of the entrance to the Jefferson County Courthouse, completed in 1932, shows some of the external Art Deco so characteristic of the building. Photo by Wesley Norton.

Above
The restored home of John Jay and Sally French, built in 1845, now houses the John Jay French Museum, maintained by the Beaumont Heritage Society. The Junior League of Beaumont bought the house in 1968 after it had been out of the hands of the French family for some time. The restoration includes furnishings and outbuildings characteristic of mid-19th century rural life in Southeast Texas. Photo by Wesley Norton.

Top
Plans for the Babe Didrikson Zaharias Memorial were formulated in 1969 by a committee headed by Ben Rogers and Thad Johnson. Ground was broken in 1975 on land donated by the city, and the building was completed a year later. Memorabilia of Beaumont's most accomplished athlete is on display for visitors and residents alike. Photo by Wesley Norton.

Above
Since 1943 the Lower Neches Valley Authority, as a state agency, has operated a water distributing system of which Dam B and Steinhagen Lake, shown here, are a part. The agency now has the capacity to pump a billion gallons per day through 400 miles of canals to rice fields, industries, and city residents, while also engaging in water pollution control. Courtesy, Lower Neches Valley Authority.

Above
A ship at the Port of Beaumont remains brightly lit throughout the night. Photo by Kenneth Linsley.

Top left
The Beaumont Public Library, dedicated September 22, 1974, is one of the most visible of the projects financed by a 1971 bond issue which also included sewer, water, and street improvements. The same bond issue provided for the Police and Municipal Court Building. Photo by Wesley Norton.

Top right
Founded in 1962, the Beaumont Civic Opera Company has presented a professional musical production every year, with

support from the Moody Foundation, the Mobil Foundation, and Carol Tyrrell Kyle, among others. Shown is the 1969 production of Donizetti's Elixir of Love, *with Mary Woodland, seated at left, singing the lead. Dr. Peter Paul Fuchs conducted and Naaman Woodland created the sets. Courtesy, Naaman Woodland.*

Middle left
Parkdale Mall, the Golden Triangle's only enclosed shopping mall, was opened October 11, 1973,

as a result of the financial initiative taken by Rogers Brothers' Enterprise. It currently houses 85 businesses. Photo by Wesley Norton.

Middle right
Future aviator Shannon Wilson poses beside one of the antique aircraft on display in an air show at Jefferson County Airport in 1981. Photo by Kenneth Linsley.

Above left
The Beaumont Fire Department has rebuilt and maintained this

ladder truck bought in 1911 as the first piece of motorized equipment for the department. It was driven under its own power to be exhibited at Spindletop Boom Days in 1981. Photo by Wesley Norton.

Above
The Jack Brooks Federal Building, located on Willow Street, houses the central post office and the federal court. Originally built in the 1930s, it has undergone extensive remodelling several times. Photo by Wesley Norton.

*Early morning sun illuminates
the color of fall on a country road
just north of Beaumont. Photo by
Wesley Norton.*

The sun sets along the upper Gulf Coast below Beaumont. Photo by Wesley Norton.

Top left
In 1907 the Texas Agricultural Experiment Station was established at Amelia, west of Beaumont, by the Texas Legislature. In cooperation with Texas A and M University, the U.S. Department of Agriculture, and the Rice Growers Association, the center is vitally involved here and throughout the world in the green revolution. Especially concerned with rice culture, the staff conducts extensive research in plant genetics, weed and disease control, and production technology. Courtesy, J.P. Craigmiles.

Top right
The new City Hall, pictured here, and the nearby Civic Center were financed by an $18 million bond issue passed by Beaumonters in 1974. Photo by Wesley Norton.

Above
This photo shows the Western Pace Setter I, one of the largest offshore drilling rigs ever built, headed for service in the North Sea. One of the major enterprises at Bethlehem Steel Shipyard in recent years has been the building and outfitting of these mammoth rigs that resemble nothing less than floating cities. Courtesy, Business Men's Studio.

Bibliography

Abernethy, Francis Edward. *Legendary Ladies of Texas.* Dallas: E-Heart Press, 1981.

Asbury, Ray. *The South Park Story 1891-1971 and the Founding of Lamar University 1923-1941.* Ft. Worth: Evans Press, Inc., 1971.

Ashford, Gerald. *Spanish Texas Yesterday and Today.* Austin: Jenkins, 1971.

Barker, Eugene C. "The African Slave Trade in Texas." *Texas Historical Association Quarterly,* VI (July 1902-April 1903).

Beaumont Chamber of Commerce. *Seventy-Fifth Anniversary Meeting Program.* January 25, 1979.

Beaumont, City of. *Minutes of Commission Meetings, 1930-1936.*

Beaumont: A Guide to the City and Its Environs. Work Projects Administration in the State of Texas, Federal Writers' Project. American Guide Series. Houston: Anson Jones Press, 1938.

Beaumont Enterprise. Scattered issues. 1880-1982.

Beaumont Journal. Scattered issues. 1895-1982.

Binkley, William C. *The Texas Revolution.* Baton Rouge: Louisiana State University Press, 1952.

Block, W.T. "Beaumont in the 1850s: Extracts from the Writings of Henry R. Green." *Texas Gulf Historical and Biographical Record,* XI (November 1975).

_____. "Charles Cronea of Sabine Pass: Lafitte Buccaneer and Texas Veteran." *Texas Gulf Historical and Biographical Record,* XI (November 1975).

_____. "Documents of the Early Sawmilling Epoch." *Texas Gulf Historical and Biographical Record,* IX (November 1973).

_____. *Emerald of the Neches: The Chronicles of Beaumont, Texas from Reconstruction to Spindletop,* Nederland Publishing Company, 1980.

_____. *A History of Jefferson County, Texas from Wilderness to Reconstruction.* Nederland Publishing Company, 1976.

_____. "The Last of Lafitte's Pirates," *Frontier Times,* LI (June-July 1977).

_____. "The Legacy of Jean Lafitte in the Neutral Strip," *True West Magazine,* XXVII (November-December 1979).

_____. "Record of the Board of Aldermen of the Town of Beaumont, 1860-1861." *Texas Gulf Historical and Biographical Record,* XI (November 1975).

_____. "The Romance of Sabine Lake." *Texas Gulf Historical and Biographical Record,* IX (November 1973).

Bolton, Herbert Eugene. *Texas in the Middle Eighteenth Century.* Austin: University of Texas Press, 1970.

Bretlinger, W. Brock. "The Contribution of the Fine Arts to the Culture of Beaumont." *Texas Gulf Historical and Biographical Record,* XVII (November 1981).

Brindley, Anne. "Jane Long." *Southwestern Historical Quarterly,* LVI (October 1952).

Burran, James A. "Violence in an Arsenal of Democracy: Beaumont Race Riot 1943." *East Texas Historical Journal,* XIV (Spring 1976).

Coyle, Joseph S. "Job Meccas for the '80s." *Money,* VII (May 1978).

Crenshaw, Rosa Dieu and W.W. Ward. *Cornerstones.* Beaumont: First Methodist Church Historical Committee, 1968.

Clark, James A. and Michel T. Halbouty. *Spindletop.* New York: Random House, 1952.

Dailey, Nancy. "History of the Beaumont, Texas Chapter of the National Association for the Advancement of Colored People, 1918-1970." Unpublished Master's thesis, Lamar University, 1971.

Dewees, William B. *Letters from an Early Settler of Texas.* Waco: Texian Press, 1968.

Doran, Michael F. (ed.). "Early Beaumont: the Reminiscences of Frank C. Weber." *Texas Gulf Historical and Biographical Record,* XVII (November 1981).

Doring, Ernest N. "The Yount Collection." *Violins,* I (April 1938).

Dutton, Genevieve Broussard. "Pioneer Rice Industrialist and Man of Faith: Joseph Eloi Broussard." *Texas Gulf Historical and Biographical Record,* XV (November 1979).

Elliott, Keith. "Beaumont: Poor Little Rich Town." Reprinted from *Texas Parade,* 1976.

Estep, W.R. *And God Gave the Increase: The Centennial History of the First Baptist Church of Beaumont, Texas, 1872-1972.* Beaumont: First Baptist Church, 1972.

Faulk, Odie B. *The Last Years of Spanish Texas.* The Hague: Mouton and Company, 1964.

Flasdyck, Alice. Unpublished Diary. Beaumont, 1920.

Fletcher, William A. *Rebel Private, Front and Rear.* Austin: University of Texas Press, 1954.

Folmer, Henri. "De Bellisle on the Texas Coast." *Southwestern Historical Quarterly,* XLIV (July 1940-April 1941).

Fornell, Earl W. *The Galveston Era.* Austin: University of Texas Press, 1961.

The French Texans. San Antonio: The Institute of Texan Cultures, 1973.

Franklin, Rogayle. "Beaumont: Modern-Day Boomtown." *Texas Business.* January 1982.

Gammel, H.P.N. *The Laws of Texas.* Vol. I. Austin: The Gammel Book Company, 1898.

General Investigating Committee Report to the House of Representatives of the Texas Legislature. 57th Legislature of Texas. Jefferson County Investigation, Vol. II. Austin, Texas, 1961.

Gray, William Fairfax. *From Virginia to Texas, 1835: Diary of Col. William F. Gray.* Houston: Gray, Dillaye & Company, Printers (Fletcher Young Publishing Co.), 1965.

Head, Richard Henry. "Public School Desegregation in Beaumont, Texas, 1954-69," Unpublished Master's thesis, Lamar University, 1970.

History and Symbolism of Saint Anthony's Church, Beaumont. Beaumont: 1943.

History of St. Mark's Parish, Beaumont, Texas. Beaumont: Lamb Printing Company, 1930.

Hogan, William Ransom. *The Texas Republic: A Social and Economic History.* Austin: University of Texas Press, 1969.

Interview with Mary Lou Ainsworth, January 13, 1982, Beaumont.

Interview with Velma White Caswell, January 25, 1982, Beaumont.

Interview with Ruth and Florence Chambers, January 10, 1982, Beaumont.

Interview with Myrtle Sprott Deplanter, January 31, 1982, Beaumont.

Interview with William Gilbert, January 17, 1982, Beaumont.

Interview with Tanner T. Hunt, February 16, 1982, Beaumont.

Interview with Robert Q. Keith, November 3, 1981, Beaumont.

Interview with Maurice Meyers, January 18, 1982, Beaumont.

Interview with Jane Clark Owens, September 8, 1981, Beaumont.

Interview with Dennis Sederholm, January 8, 1982, Beaumont.

Interview with Mamie McFaddin Ward, February 3, 1982, Beaumont.

Isaac, Paul E. "A History of the Charters of Beaumont, Texas, 1838-1947." *Mirabeau B. Lamar Series in Urban Affairs.* I. Beaumont Center for Urban Affairs, Lamar University, n.d.

The Italian Texans. The Texians and Texans. Pamphlet Series. San Antonio: Institute of Texan Cultures, 1973.

Johnson, Thelma, et al. *The Spindletop Oil Field, A History of Its Discovery and Development.* Beaumont: George W. Norvell, 1927.

The Journal of Jean Laffite: The Privateer-Patriot's Own Story. New York: Vantage Press, Inc., 1958.

Kroutter, Thomas E. "The Ku Klux Klan in Jefferson County, Texas, 1921-1924." Unpublished Master's thesis, Lamar University, 1972.

Laird, Gary. "Beaumont: The Victorian Experience in Architecture." Unpublished Master's thesis, Lamar University, 1971.

McDonald, Archie P., (ed.). *Eastern Texas History.* Austin: Jenkins Publishing Company, 1978.

Meinig, Donald W. *Imperial Texas.* Austin: University of Texas Press, 1969.

Morfi, Fray Juan Agustín. *History of Texas, 1673-1779.* New York: Arno Press, 1967.

Newcomb, W.W., Jr. *The Indians of Texas.* Austin: University of Texas Press, 1961.

Olmsted, Frederick Law. *A Journey through Texas.* Austin: University of Texas Press, 1978.

Osburn, Mary McMillan (ed.). "The Atascocito Census of 1826." *Texana,* I (Fall 1963).

Parigi, Sam F., and Clara Jo Liberto. "The Italian-Americans of Southeast Texas." *Texas Gulf Historical and Biographical Record,* XVI (November 1980).

Parker, Dr. George. *Oil Field Medico.* Dallas: Banks Upshaw and Company, 1948.

Partlow, Miriam. *Liberty, Liberty County, and the Atascocito District.* Austin: Pemberton Press, 1974.

Pichardo, Jose Antonio. *Pichardo's Treatise on the Limits of Louisiana and Texas.* Vol. III. Austin: University of Texas Press, 1941.

Polk's Morrison & Fourmy Beaumont (Texas) City Directory, 1931. Houston: Morrison & Fourmy Directory Company, Inc., 1931.

Proceedings of a Convention of Delegates, Chosen by the People of Massachusetts, without Distinction of Party, . . . to Take Into Consideration the Proposed Annexation of Texas to the United States. Published by order of the Convention. Boston: Eastburn's Press, 1845.

Pulsifer, Joseph. Unpublished papers, 1835-1836.

Ragan, Cooper K. "The Diary of Captain George W. O'Brien, 1863." *Southwestern Historical Quarterly,* LXVII (July 1963).

Richardson, Rupert Norval, Ernest Wallace, and Adrian N. Anderson. *Texas: The Lone Star State.* Englewood Cliffs, New Jersey: Prentice-Hall, Inc., 1981.

Robinson, Jeanette Heard. "Beaumont's Golden Era for the Performing Arts: 1925-1931." Unpublished Master's thesis, Lamar

University, 1976.

Saxon, Lyle. *Lafitte, the Pirate.* New Orleans: Robert L. Crager and Company, 1950.

Seale, William. *Texas Riverman.* Austin: University of Texas Press, 1966.

Simons, Vivian Yevetta. "The Prohibition Movement in Beaumont, Texas, 1835-1919." Unpublished Master's thesis, Lamar University, 1963.

Solís, Fray Gaspar José de, "Diary of a Visit of Inspection of the Texas Missions Made by Fray Gaspar Jose de Solis in the Year 1767-68." *Southwestern Historical Quarterly,* XXXV (July 1931-April 1932).

Spindletop: Where Oil Became an Industry. Spindletop 50th Anniversary Commission. 1951.

The Standard Blue Book of Texas: Edition de Luxe of Beaumont. Houston: the A.J. Peeler Standard Blue Book Company of Texas, 1908-1909.

Stratton, Florence. *The Story of Beaumont.* Beaumont: 1927.

Tevis, Reid W., and Nancy Snyder Speer. "Nancy Tevis (1796-1876)." from *Women in Early Texas.* Austin: Jenkins, 1975.

Touchet, Robert W. "New Deal Work Programs in Jefferson County, Texas: The Civilian Conservation Corps at Tyrrell Park." Unpublished Master's thesis, Lamar

University, 1972.

Trevey, Marilyn Dianne Stodgehill. "The Social and Economic Impact of the Spindletop Oil Boom on Beaumont in 1901." Unpublished Master's thesis, Lamar University, 1974.

Weinbaum, Eleanor Perlstein. *Shalom, America.* San Antonio: Naylor Company, 1969.

Welch, Joe Ben. "A History of the Growth and Development of Lamar University from 1949 to 1973." Unpublished Master's thesis, McNeese University, Lake Charles, Louisiana, 1974.

Welch, June Rayfield. *Historic Sites of Texas.* Waco: Texian Press, 1972.

Wilson, Rosine McFaddin. "The McFaddin Family." *Texas Gulf Historical and Biographical Record,* XVI (November 1980).

_____. "Spaniards to Spindletop." Series of articles printed in *Beaumont Enterprise,* November 1966.

Woodhead, Ben. *Beaumonter at Large.* Beaumont: 1968.

Wooster, Ralph A. *The Secession Conventions of the South.* Princeton: Princeton University Press, 1962.

_____. "The Texas Gulf Coast in the Civil War." *Texas Gulf Historical and Biographical Record,* I (November 1965).

Zaharias, Babe Didrikson. *This Life I've Led.* New York: Dell Publishing Company, Inc., 1955.

This unidentified young lady portends a new decade as she poses in front of gingerbread Victorian homes and automobiles of the 1920s. These eclectic homes on Elizabeth Street belonged to Mr. and Mrs. George Cheesman and Mr. and Mrs. George W. Smyth. The Smyth home on the right was used as a hospital and then a hotel before its demolition. Courtesy, Ruth and Florence Chambers.

Index

Judith Linsley and Ellen Rienstra share many things besides their maiden name of Walker. The sisters are sixth-generation Beaumonters, descendants of early Beaumont merchant John Jay French and several area pioneer families. Both women earned their bachelor and master of arts degrees from Lamar University (Judith in Spanish and history, respectively, Ellen in English literature), and both have an abiding interest in Beaumont history.

Mrs. Linsley brings to this book the perspective and skill of a serious, longtime student of local history. During her work for the master's degree, she wrote "The Election of 1908 in Texas," "Merchants in the Trans-Mississippi South, 1845-1860," and "Spindletop and Religion in Beaumont." Her thesis is entitled *A Social History of Beaumont in the 1920s* and deals with a pivotal period in Beaumont's development.

"A Family Full of Legends" is the name of an article written by Mrs. Rienstra that appeared in *Tales From the Big Thicket,* edited by Francis E. Abernethy and published by the University of Texas Press. Ellen Rienstra is known for her involvement in Beaumont history, having served as a researcher for the Beaumont Heritage Society's restoration project, the John Jay French trading post. She also was instrumental in initiating the society's educational program. Mrs. Rienstra has lectured on various aspects of Beaumont history to groups in the community.

Before embarking on *Beaumont: A Chronicle of Promise,* the sisters collaborated on an article on the Cajun influence in Texas for *Antiques USA* magazine, and a booklet for the Beaumont Heritage Society entitled *Music in Texas—Frontier to 1900.* They both are members of the Texas Folklore Society and charter members of the Beaumont Heritage Society; Mrs. Linsley also belongs to the Southeast Texas Genealogical and Historical Society.